# EVOLUTIONARY ILLUSTRATION OF CHINESE CHARACTERS

Written and sketched by Li Leyi
Translated by Jiang Lizhu

Beijing Language and Culture University Press

北京语言文化大学出版社

（京）新登字 157 号

**图书在版编目（CIP）数据**

汉字演变五百例续编：英文版/李乐毅著；蒋立珠译 .
—北京：北京语言文化大学出版社，2000
ISBN 7 – 5619 – 0852 – 0

Ⅰ . 汉…

Ⅱ .①李…　②蒋…

Ⅲ . 汉字－演变－英文

Ⅳ . H12

中国版本图书馆 CIP 数据核字（2000）第 04384 号

责任印制：乔学军
出版发行：北京语言文化大学出版社
　　　　　（北京海淀区学院路 15 号　邮政编码 100083）
印　　刷：北京北林印刷厂
经　　销：全国新华书店
版　　次：2000 年 9 月第 1 版　2000 年 9 月第 1 次印刷
开　　本：850 毫米×1168 毫米　1/32　印张：16.75
字　　数：215 千字　印数：0001 – 3000
书　　号：ISBN 7 – 5619 – 0852 – 0/H·0027
定　　价：25.00 元

# Publisher's Note

In 1992, the book entitled *Tracing the Roots of Chinese Characters : 500 Cases*, written and sketched by Professor Li Leyi, was published by the Press and in the following year it was translated into the versions of English, French and German. Presenting not only a vivid delineation of both graphs and words but also a method of making profound ideas into simple terms, the book tried every effort to make the characters research more visualized and popularized, hence, it received a warm welcome from the readers domestic and abroad.

As for this newly published book, *Evolutionary Illustration of Chinese Characters*, should be regarded as "a continuation" of the former, as it were, another "500 Cases". Minded readers must have noticed that the "continuation" has made some changes comparing to the former and it is unnecessary to mention them in details here for the capacity limit. The author and the Press sincerely look forward to receiving any criticism and suggestions.

Beijing Language and Culture University Press

January 2000

# CONTENTS

# Preface

The Chinese character is one of the earliest forms of written language in the world. Even though it has an evolution history of approximately five or six thousand years, probably one-fourth of the world's population are still using it now. The Chinese character has made a great contribution to the development of China's long standing cultural history. As an art form, the graceful Chinese calligraphy is an indispensable part of the cultural and artistic legacy of the Chinese nation.

The past several thousands of years have witnessed the evolution of Chinese characters, of which the main forms are as follows:

## I. *Jia Gu Wen* : Oracle Bone Inscriptions

*Jian gu wen* refers to the writings inscribed on the carapaces of tortoises and on mammal animals during the Shang Dynasty (c.16th − 11th century B.C.). Because it mainly recorded the art of divination, it was called *bu ci*, divination writings, or *qi wen*, inscribed writings. As the inscriptions were firstly discovered in the Yin ruins (the capital ruins from the end of the Shang Dynasty, now Xiaotun Village, Anyang County, Henan Province), were also known as "Yin ruins characters." One thousand or of the over four thousand characters inscribed on the collected bones can be deciphered and understood. Although to some his ancient script is a set language, many strokes and radinot in a final fixed form. In the early period of the Zhou y (c. 11th − 256 B.C.), some oracle bones were already unearthed.

## II. *Jin Wen*: **Bronze Inscriptions**

The characters cast or inscribed on the bronze articles of the Shang and Zhou dynasties are known as *jin wen*, or *zhong ding wen* (writings on bronze bells or tripods). The earliest was similar to the oracle bone inscriptions, some of which even retained the form of the early pictographs. The latest was closer in form to the descendant, *xiao zhuan*, small seal characters. Over two thousand of the nearly four thousand collected single characters on the bronze objects can be deciphered and understood. The forms and structures of *jin wen* show a much greater maturity than the predecessors, and the text inscribed on one bronze object in the Zhou Dynasty runs as long as five hundred characters.

## III. *Xiao Zhuan*: **Small Seal Characters**

It is the written language popularly used in the Qin Dynasty (221 – 207 B.C.). It is also known as *Qin zhuan*, Qin Dynasty characters. During the Warring States Period (475 – 221 B.C.), different writings were in use in different parts of the land. Following the conquest and unification of the country, the first emperor of the Qin Dynasty simplified and unified the written language. Based on *da zhuan*, big seal characters, which was also called *z* *wen*, characters popularly used in the Qin State during the S and Autumn (770 – 476 B.C.) and the Warring States Peri newly standard form of characters, *xiao zhuan*, small seal ters, came into being. The unification of the written lang the Qin Dynasty contributed significantly to the standardiz the Chinese character.

## IV. *Li Shu* : Official Script

As a formal written language in the Han Dynasty (206 B.C. – 220 A.D.), this form came into use at the end of the Qin Dynasty, and lasted to the Three Kingdoms Period (220 – 280 A.D.). It is also called *Han li*, Han Dynasty script, and other names. In the early versions of official script, traces of small seal characters can still be observed. However, in the later versions, curved and broken strokes gradually increased, which became a distinct characteristic of official script. As a sound foundation laid for the coming standardization of Chinese characters, official script symbolized a turning point in the evolution history of Chinese characters. Since that time, the Chinese character has moved from an ancient time to a modern stage of development.

## V. *Kai Shu* : Regular Script

Appearing at the end of the Han Dynasty, *kai shu* has been in vogue to the present day and still in common use. It is characterized by a straight and upright character form, which can be thought of a model, and thus is also named *zheng shu*, square script, and *zhen shu*, realistic script. In history, many calligraphers are famous for their use of *kai shu* in their artistic creations.

## VI. *Cao Shu* : Cursive Writing *or* Grass Stroke Characters

Appearing first at the beginning of the Han Dynasty, *cao shu* was actually a much earlier form than *kai shu*. The earliest cursive writings were variants of the rapid free-style written form of official script, and they were called *cao li*, cursive official script. Later, they became known as *zhang cao*, cursive seal characters. Since the end of the Han Dynasty, with the traces retained in the cursive seal characters no longer visible, *jin cao*, contemporary cursive script, of which the strokes became uninterrupted and the radicals mutually interchangeable, began to emerge. In the Tang Dynasty (618 – 907 A.D.), another form of *cao shu* evolved into *kuang cao*, "extreme" cursive script, with strokes becoming more unorthodox and some characters even illegible. The cursive calligraphy used at the present day is generally in the form of *jin cao*.

### VII. *Xing Shu*: Freehand Cursive *or* Running Hand

As a writing between *kai shu* and *cao shu*, it appeared and became popular during the Three Kingdoms Period and the Jin Dynasty (265 – 420 A.D.). Such a form is more convenient to write than *kai shu* and easier to read than *cao shu*, so it became the preferred writing style of people. *Xing shu* can also be divided into two categories: *xing kai* and *xing cao*. The former is composed of more orthodox strokes, while the latter tends more toward employing more cursive style strokes. Their difference, however, is not readily apparent.

In addition, since the birth of the Chinese written language a great number of simplified versions of characters emerged for the convenience of usage. They were called *su zi*, common characters, *shou tou zi*, "handy characters," etc. In the development process of Chinese characters, there existed tendencies both to complicate and to simplify, of which the latter was the main current. Though the simplified characters once appeared in ancient times, only in the 1950s the simplified characters popular throughout Chinese history were systematically researched and arranged in mainland China, and hence several waves of "simplified characters" were issued, which have become the normal ones in use today.

Aiming to promote the general readers' understanding of the evolution of Chinese characters and make them better aware of traditional Chinese culture as well, the book is written and compiled with the following features:

1. This is a common book concerning Chinese characters for the average readers. It is the continuation of *Tracing the Roots of Chinese Characters : 500 Cases*. With a list of some versions of several main Chinese character forms, each one is presented with a vivid picture and a simple explanation, tying to describe simply and visually the evolutionary history of Chinese characters.

2. With the characters not included in the former book, another 500 Chinese ones (more than 600 characters if one includes the interchangeable words, loan words and others) have been selected in the book. Each character is presented in each of its seven forms: oracle bone inscriptions, bronze inscriptions, small seal characters, official script, regular script, grass stroke characters, and freehand cursive writing (some have been simplified; if the simplified versions of *kai shu* added, altogether eight forms). Some particular versions of *jin wen* are replaced by *zhou wen* or Warring States Period characters.

3. Some Chinese characters in certain forms can be written in a multitude of ways. Examples selected in this book are the comparatively typical and commonly used ones. The origins are omitted for convenience.

4. The philological explanation is based on the generally accepted conclusions of philologists, the conclusions of some schools of thought, and the author's view as well. Due to the limited capacity of this book, the explanations are not fully elaborated and the source books are not listed.

5. The texts are arranged in the alphabetical order based on the *pin yin* system (characters with more than one pronunciation are arranged based on their more common usage).

# Index of Hanyu Pinyin

(Characters in parentheses are complex forms;
characters in square brackets are interchangeable forms.)

侧（側）cè　　　　　　　33

差 chā,chà,chāi,cī　　34

　[搓 cuō 磋 cuō]

屠 chán　　　　　　35

产（産）chǎn　　　　36

常 cháng　　　　　　37

[裳 shang,cháng]

昶 chǎng　　　　　　38

畅 chàng　　　　　　39

　[畅（暢）chàng]

巢 cháo　　　　　　40

彻（徹）chè　　　　41

　[撤 chè 澈 chè]

尘（塵）chén　　　　42

城 chéng　　　　　　43

尺 chǐ　　　　　　　44

崇 chóng　　　　　　45

　[嵩 sōng 崧 sōng]

畴（疇）chóu　　　　46

　[寿（壽）shòu 俦（儔）chóu]

雠（讎）chóu　　　　47

　[仇 chóu]

丑（醜）chǒu　　　　48

臭 chòu,xiù　　　　49

　[嗅 xiù]

处（處）chǔ,chù　　50

穿 chuān　　　　　　51

窗 chuāng　　　　　52

　[囱 cōng]

创（創 剙）chuāng,chuàng　　53

床（牀）chuáng　　　　54

　[爿 pán]

垂 chuí　　　　　　　55

　[陲 chuí]

刺 cì　　　　　　　　56

粗 cū　　　　　　　　57

毳 cuì　　　　　　　58

　[脆 cuì 橇 qiāo]

寸 cùn　　　　　　　59

D

逮 dài　　　　　　　60

弹（彈）dàn,tán　　　61

道 dào　　　　　　　62

　[导（導）dǎo]

到 dào　　　　　　　

　[倒 dǎo,dào]　　　63

盗 dào　　　　　　　64

低 dī　　　　　　　　65

　[氐 dī 柢 dī 底 dǐ]

翟 dí,Zhái　　　　66

弟 dì　　　　　　　67

　[第 dì 悌 tì]

甸 diàn　　　　　　

　[佃 diàn]　　　　68

吊（弔）diào　　　　69

　[叔 shū 淑 shū]

定 dìng　　　　　　70

· 12 ·

# Index of Strokes

(Arranged according to the number of strokes and 一 丨 丿 、 ﹁; characters in bold face are basic ones and the others are interchangeable forms, etc.)

· 23 ·

| | | | | | | |
|---|---|---|---|---|---|
| 搜 | 344 | 善 | 299 | 微 | 367 |
| 煮 | 328 | 粪(糞) | 94 | 愈 | 443 |
| 搓 | 34 | 湿(濕 溼) | 310 | 肆 | 428 |
| 斯 | 337 | 游(遊) | 438 | [、]韵 | 191 |
| 散 | 293 | 曾 | 469 | 意 | 426 |
| 葬 | 461 | 寒 | 123 | 雍 | 436 |
| 戟 | 153 | 富 | 103 | 源 | 452 |
| 朝 | 473 | 窗 | 52 | 拳 | 138 |
| 森 | 295 | 裕 | 449 | 猷 | 439 |
| 焚 | 92 | [一]屏 | 35 | 粱 | 214 |
| 椠 | 195 | 媚 | 240 | 煅 | 73 |
| 惠 | 140 | 鼍 | 485 | 煌 | 139 |
| 粟 | 346 | 编(編) | 20 | [一]辟₁ | 19 |
| 棘 | 151 | | | 辟₂(闢) | 264 |
| 雁 | 415 | **13 strokes** | | | |
| [丨]最 | 498 | | | **14 strokes** | |
| 量 | 215 | [一]瑟 | 294 | [一]墙(墙 牆) | 276 |
| 畴(疇) | 46 | 裛 | 329 | 嘉 | 157 |
| 蛛 | 489 | 零 | 222 | 赫 | 126 |
| 帽 | 237 | [丨]盟 | 241 | 境 | 178 |
| 黑 | 127 | 照 | 475 | 蒇(巉) | 247 |
| [丿]短 | 72 | 嗣 | 339 | 蔗 | 478 |
| 毳 | 58 | 嗅 | 49 | 兢 | 176 |
| 焦 | 169 | 遣 | 274 | 碾 | 73 |
| 番 | 85 | 罪 | 499 | 磋 | 34 |
| 腑 | 101 | 罩 | 495 | [丨]裳 | 37 |
| 然 | 285 | 嵩 | 45 | 罴(羆) | 4 |
| [、]敦 | 75 | [丿]稚 | 155 | [丿]锻(鍛) | 73 |
| 童 | 360 | 筮 | 316 | 熏(薰 燻) | 407 |
| 羡 | 388 | 简(簡) | 161 | 箸 | 492 |
| 道 | 62 | 鼠 | 326 | 僮 | 360 |

· 28 ·

# 哀 āi

Quite different from most characters with the radical of 衣, 衣 in this character has no literal meaning but is only a symbol to indicate sound. The original meaning of 哀 is "to take pity on," and its extended meaning is "to sorrow."

（缺）

金文

小篆

隶书

楷书

草书

行书

简化字

（同楷书）

1

# 爱（愛）ài

Initially, it was written as 悉.
Graphically, it looked like a person who
was holding a 心 (heart) with his two
hands and recounting love from the bottom of his heart with his mouth widely
open.

（缺）

金文

小篆

隶书

楷书

草书

行书

简化字

# 岸 àn

This character was originally written as 厂, meaning the edge of both mountains and waters. Later, a phonetic symbol 干 was added and it became 厈. Finally, a significance symbol 山, mountain, was added, hence it came into the form of 岸. The original meaning is "the high lands by the waters."

（缺）

岸
岸
岸
岸
岸

（同楷书）

# 罢（罷）bà

〔附〕罴（羆）pí

It was the original form of 罴. The character's upper part is 网, net; the lower part is 能, meaning 熊 (see character 能). 罴, a kind of bear, is called 人熊 or 马熊, brown bear, whose gall-bladder could be used as a medicine material so it was usually hunted by people. In later days, it was mostly loaned to mean 罢免, to dismiss, 停止, to stop or cease, etc.

4

# 百 bǎi

百, since it appeared in oracle bone inscriptions, has functioned as a numeral. For its pronunciation similar to that of 白 (bái), a plane was added to the top, in this way 百 was formed. In ancient scripts, it also indicated "a multitude in numbers," such as 百废具兴, full-scale construction is under way, 百家争鸣, a hundred schools of thought contend.

（同楷书）

5

# 拜 bài

It is a formality to show one's respect. The original form should be like this: two hands were put palm to palm for saluting, because some ancient forms of the character were just written like this. However, since small seal characters, its strokes differed left and right from its former one.

（缺）

（同楷书）

甲骨文

三体石经

小篆

隶书

楷书

草书

行书

简化字

6

# 班 bān

The initial meaning was "to cut a jade into two halves." In bronze inscriptions, it graphically looked like a knife cutting two strings of jades（玉）. It extended to mean "to divide," "to publicize," "sequence," etc.

甲骨文

（缺）

金文

班

班

小篆

班

隶书

班

楷书

班

草书

行书

（同楷书）

简化字

7

# 半 bàn

Originally, the upper part of the character was 八, to divide, and the lower part 牛. Together it signified to divide a cow or ox in the middle, i.e. 一半, a half. The extended meaning is "in the middle of," such as 半夜, midnight, 半路, half way.

甲骨文

金文

小篆

隶书

楷书

草书

行书

简化字

# 伴 bàn

In oracle bone inscriptions, it was like two people（大）shoulder to shoulder playing. With the time going, it evolved into two 夫, man. 伴 once appeared in small seal characters, but meant 胖, fat. It was also loaned to indicate 伴侣, company.

甲骨文　林

金文　（缺）

小篆　林

隶书　伴

楷书　伴

草书　伴

行书　伴

简化字　（同楷书）

# 包 bāo

〔附〕胞 bāo 苞 bāo

It was the original form of 胞. Later, it was mostly used to mean 包裹, wrap up, 包含, include, 包容, contain, etc., hence 胞 was coined to convey its original sense. With the indication of grass or trees, another character 苞 was originated.

甲骨文

金文

小篆

隶书

楷书

草书

行书

简化字

（同楷书）

10

# 暴 bào

〔附〕曝 pù

It was the original form of 曝, and firstly appeared on Zhong Shan King Tripod（中山王鼎）of the Spring and Autumn and the Warring States Periods. In small seal characters, its grapheme was two hands holding a farming implement and drying rice in the sun. The original meaning was 晒, to sun.

（缺）

（同楷书）

# 报 （報） bào

The original meaning was "to declare guilty." In oracle bone inscriptions, the grapheme was vividly delineated: a big hand was holding a prisoner and handcuffing him (see character 幸).

甲骨文 金文 小篆 隶书 楷书 草书 行书 简化字

# 卑 bēi

It meant "humble or in a low status" originally. The character was not found in oracle bone inscriptions, but in bronze inscriptions, its form was like a slave's hand with a big fan serving his master. It had the extended meanings of "inferior," "courtesy," etc.

（同楷书）

13

# 备（備）bèi

It was the initial form of 箙（also as 葡）. Its initial meaning was "an equipment to place arrows." The grapheme in oracle bone inscriptions was a container with one or two arrows（representing many）inside. In bronze inscriptions, the radical 人 was added. With the indication of abundant weapons, it contained a meaning of 齐备, to get ready with something.

甲骨文
金文
小篆
隶书
楷书
草书
行书
简化字

# 奔 bēn

The upper part is the graph of a man running fast with his arms fully stretched, and the lower three feet (止, i.e. 趾), emphasizing a high speed. The original meaning was "running fast." Its extended meaning was 逃亡, to go into exile.

甲骨文

金文

小篆

隶书

楷书

草书

行书

简化字

（同楷书）

15

# 本 běn

The original meaning is "the root of a tree." Though invisible in oracle bone inscriptions, the character was like a tree with a small dot on its root, symbolizing where the root was. Later, it extended to signify "the stem of grass or the trunk of wood," or "the foundation or the main body of something," etc.

金文

小篆

隶书

楷书

草书

行书

简化字

（同楷书）

16

# 匕 bǐ

〔附〕妣 bǐ

It was a utensil for getting food and its shape resembled a spoon, from which the modern spoons in later generations were originated. In oracle bone inscriptions and bronze inscriptions, it was mostly loaned as 妣; it was also used as a symbol for female animals.

（同楷书）

17

# 闭（閉）bì

The character was not found in oracle bone inscriptions. In bronze inscriptions, it was like two doors with a latch in between, indicating "to close the door." Since small seal characters, the form of 十 mistakenly went into 才, which became very incomprehensible.

（缺）

| 甲骨文 | 金文 | 小篆 | 隶书 | 楷书 | 草书 | 行书 | 简化字 |
|---|---|---|---|---|---|---|---|

# 辟₁ bì, pì

〔附〕避 bì 壁 bì 璧 bì 臂 pì

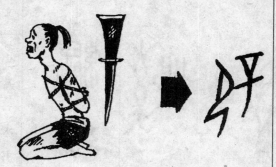

The original meaning was 法, law. In oracle bone inscriptions, its grapheme was to punish a lawbreaker with a punishment knife. In ancient scripts, 辟 was widely in use, and it was interchangeable with 避, 壁, 璧, 臂, etc. See also character 辟₂.

| | |
|---|---|
| 甲骨文 | 𤔲 |
| 金文 | 辟 |
| 小篆 | 辟 |
| 隶书 | 辟 |
| 楷书 | 辟 |
| 草书 | 辟 |
| 行书 | 辟 |
| 简化字 | （同楷书） |

19

# 编 (編) biān

The earliest form of the character was composed of 糸 and 册, indicating to thread *zu jian*, bamboo slips, into 册 with ropes. Its original meaning was "the ropes linking bamboo slips." It also referred to "sequence in order," such as 编年, chronicle, 编号, number.

（缺）

20

# 扁 biǎn

〔附〕匾 biǎn

The original meaning was "to inscribe characters on both sides of or above the door." In the later days, it was written as 匾. Hence, in the modern Chinese language, there are 匾额, an inscribed board，牌匾, a signboard and other items.

（同楷书）

| 甲骨文 |
| 金文 |
| 小篆 |
| 隶书 |
| 楷书 |
| 草书 |
| 行书 |
| 简化字 |

21

# 弁 biàn

It originally meant 帽子, cap or hat. The earlier form appeared to be a pair of hands supporting the hat. In ancient times, there were terms of 爵弁, a hat worn by civil officials, 皮弁, a hat worn by military officials, and others. Therefore, military officials were also named 武弁.

籀文

小篆

隶书

楷书

草书

行书

简化字

（同楷书）

# 彪 biāo

The original meaning was "the strips on a tiger." In bronze inscriptions, it took the shape of a tiger with several slanting strokes beside its back, indicating the color of the strips.

（缺）

（同楷书）

甲骨文
金文
小篆
隶书
楷书
草书
行书
简化字

表 biǎo

Its original meaning was "an outer garment." Graphically in small seal characters, the outer was 衣, the clothes, and the middle was 毛, the fur. Before the weaving of flax cloth was invented, the ancient people had made their clothes by weaving animals' leather. Therefore, the character was formed of "clothes" and "fur." The extended meaning is 外面, outside, 外表, appearance, etc.

金文

小篆

隶书

楷书

草书

行书

简化字

（同楷书）

# 别 bié

〔附〕彆 biè

It originally signified 分剖, to cut open. In oracle bone inscriptions, its grapheme was 刀, knife, on one side and 咼, bones, on the other. It was loaned to indicate 分别, to depart, 离别, to farewell. The simplified version 别 also substitutes for 彆 (biè).

（同楷书）

# 冰 bīng

〔附〕凝 níng

When the floating ice blocks come into collision with each other, the reverse V-shape is often formed. In oracle bone inscriptions, such two ices were loaned to constitute of the character 冰. Since bronze inscriptions, the radical 水 was added to its forms. In ancient times, it was interchangeable with 凝, congeal.

甲骨文

金文

小篆

隶书

楷书

草书

行书

简化字

（同楷书）

26

# 病 bìng

Originally it was 疒, illness. Graphically in oracle bone inscriptions, it was like a man lying in bed sweating (the forms of 人 and 床 were both vertically written). Subsequently, the radical 丙 was added to indicate sound. In ancient times, a light illness was called 疾, and a serious one called 病. 疒 is also pronounced nè.

甲骨文

金文

小篆

隶书

楷书

草书

行书

简化字

（同楷书）

27

# 剥（剝）bō, bāo

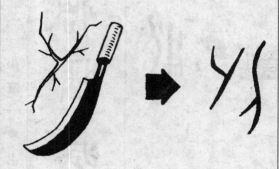

With the forms of 刀 and 卜 the character was originated, of which the former indicated meaning and the latter indicated both meaning (representing a crack) and sound. Later, it changed to take the forms of 刀 and 彖 (as a phonetic symbol). The original significance was 割裂, to cut apart. The extended meanings were 削, to cut, 去皮, to peel off, 脱落, to come off, 掠夺, to rob, etc.

28

# 帛 bó

The original meaning was 白缯, white clothing, formed by 白 and 巾, of which the former indicated meaning and the latter indicated both meaning and sound. Later, it was used for a general term for all the clothing.

（同楷书）

# 布 bù

〔附〕佈 bù

In regular script, although the character has only five strokes, it turned out to be a phonogram actually. In bronze inscriptions, it was composed of 巾 (indicating meaning) and 父 (as a phonetic symbol). However, this kind of structure is difficult to recognize in the later days. The earliest cloth referred to flax and kudzu clothing. Today, it has replaced 佈.

（缺）

（同楷书）

甲骨文　金文　小篆　隶书　楷书　草书　行书　简化字

30

# 残（殘）cán

〔附〕戋（戔）jiān

The original character was 戋（戔）, like two 戈（an ancient weapon）taking the form of pointing one another. The primitive meaning was 伤害, to hurt, or to injure. Later, 歹 was added as a semantic symbol, and its significance became obvious to guess. It can extend to mean "to kill," "to destroy," "fierce and cruel," "deformity," etc.

# 草 cǎo

The grapheme in oracle bone inscriptions was apparently a piece of grass (屮, also sounded hè). Later, it gradually evolved into the form of two pieces of grass side by side (i.e. 艸). After that, 早 was added to indicate sound. In regular script, the radical 草字头, ⺿ contained four strokes, and today's normal character has three strokes (艹).

甲骨文

金文

小篆

隶书

楷书

草书

行书

简化字

（同楷书）

# 侧 （側） cè

（缺）

Since small seal characters, it is certain to draw a conclusion that the character is composed of 人 and 则 （a phonetic symbol）. But from bronze inscriptions, it was shown that there was a large tripod （鼎） in the middle and two persons （人） on each side, just meaning 旁边, side. Later, 鼎 changed into 贝, shellfish, and 人 on the right to 刀, knife.

甲骨文

金文

小篆

隶书

楷书

草书

行书

简化字

33

# 差 chā, chà, chāi, cī

〔附〕搓 cuō 磋 cuō

The upper part of the character in bronze inscriptions was a stalk of wheat, and the lower part a hand（手, the same as 又）. The original meaning was "to peel off the wheat grains," or "grind." Subsequently，又 mistakenly converted to 左 or 右, which is not understandable. The character had ten strokes（差）in regular script as a primitive one, but today it has nine strokes（差）.

（缺）

甲骨文

金文

小篆

隶书

楷书

草书

行书

简化字

（同楷书）

# 孱 chán

It meant 懦弱, weak or coward originally. The grapheme in bronze inscriptions was quite a vivid picture: under an adult were three children so frightened that they appeared to be falling over. The extended meanings are "inferior," "cautious," etc.

35

# 产 （産）chǎn

The character was composed of 生, giving birth to, or producing（indicating the significance）, and 彦（indicating sound and its simplified form. See character 彦）. The primitive meaning was "to give birth to a son." Its extended meanings are 出生, birth, 生产, give birth to, or produce, 产品, product, 产业, industry, 财产, property, etc.

甲骨文

金文

小篆

隶书

楷书

草书

行书

简化字

# 常 cháng

〔附〕裳 shang, cháng

常 was the initial form of 裳, clothes. With the initial meaning of "an underwear," it also referred to the general clothes. It was constituted of 尚 (indicating sound) and 巾 (indicating meaning). 裳 is a variant version of the character. Later, 常 was loaned to mean 恒久, everlasting, 经常, often, 普通, common, etc., and these two characters were separated to represent the significance of their own.

# 昶 chǎng

It originally signified "a long daytime." In bronze inscriptions, it was constituted of 日 and 永, of which the former indicated the time and the latter the long period （永）. This is an associate compound character （formed by combining two or more elements, each with a meaning of its own, to create a new meaning）.

（缺）

甲骨文

金文

小篆

隶书

楷书

草书

行书

简化字

（同楷书）

38

# 鬯 chàng

〔附〕畅（暢）chàng

Originally, it was "a kind of fragrant wine for sacrificial offering or feast." The wine（denoted by a vessel）was brewed by *yu ji cao*, tulip grass（denoted by a cross sign）and black millet（denoted by little dots）. And it was also interchangeable with 畅, meaning flourishing.

（同楷书）

39

# 巢 cháo

It originally meant "a nest on the tree." According to *Suo Wen*, an ancient book on Chinese characters, birds' nest in a tree was called 巢 and in a cave was 窠. In bronze inscriptions, the upper was a nest graph and the lower a tree graph; in small seal characters, the graph of three nestlings was added above the nest and the character became more graphic.

（缺）

（同楷书）

甲骨文

金文

小篆

隶书

楷书

草书

行书

简化字

40

# 彻 (徹) chè

〔附〕撤 chè 澈 chè

The grapheme in oracle bone inscriptions was a hand on one side and a food utensil（鬲）on the other, symbolizing "to take the utensil away after dinner." In ancient writings, it was interchangeable with 撤, withdraw, and 澈, clear. The simplified character is 彻.

甲骨文

金文

小篆

隶书

楷书

草书

行书

简化字

41

# 尘（塵）chén

The earliest form of the character was a graph of three deer and two dust heaps, which indicated the flying dust raised by a group of fast running deer. In official script, the character was simplified to be one 鹿, deer, and one 土, dust. The present simplified character is composed of 小 above 土.

# 城 chéng

The left part of 城 in bronze inscriptions was mostly written as 庸（i.e. 墉）and also occasionally written as 土；the right part was 成（a phonetic radical）, or simplified as 戌. The original meaning was "the defense walls around the compact community," the interior wall was called 城, and the exterior was 郭.

甲骨文

金文

小篆

隶书

楷书

草书

行书

简化字

（同楷书）

# 尺 chǐ

The ancient people used to measure the length with their various parts of the body. For instance, 寸, the Chinese inch, was the distance from the edge of palm to the place where a pulse could be felt, and the further length to elbow was 尺, ten inches. The character of 尺 was composed of 尸（人）, body and a denotative symbol（a dot or a stroke）.

（缺）

甲骨文

金文

小篆

隶书

楷书

草书

行书

简化字

（同楷书）

44

# 崇 chóng

〔附〕嵩 sōng 崧 sōng

"High and lofty mountains" was the original meaning of the character. The extended significance referred to "the height of common things." 嵩 and 崧 were both the variants of 崇. In the later days, 嵩 especially referred to 嵩山, the middle high mountain in Henan Province today.

（缺）

甲骨文

三体石经

小篆

隶书

楷书

草书

行书

简化字

（同楷书）

45

# 畴（疇）chóu

〔附〕寿（壽）shòu 俦（儔）chóu

The original meaning was "the fields already ploughed." Its form, in oracle bone inscriptions, was like a ploughed ridge in the field with cattle's hoof prints on both sides. With the meanings of 种类, category, and 同类, congener, the character was also written as 俦. The primitive form of the character was also loaned to be 寿.

46

甲骨文

金文

小篆

隶书

楷书

草书

行书

简化字

# 雠（讎）chóu

〔附〕仇 chóu

Two birds（隹）were saying（言）with each other. It originally meant 对答, to reply one another. The extended meanings are 相等, equality, 报复, revenge, 酬偿, reward, 校勘, collating, etc. Sometimes it was interchangeable with 仇, foe.

（缺）

# 丑（醜）chǒu

丑 in oracle bone and bronze inscriptions was like a bird's claw. In ancient scripts, 爪, claw, also meant the fingernails or toenails. Hence, it was reasonable to believe it looked like a hand's shape (*Suo Wen*). Later, it was loaned to indicate the second of the Earthly Branches. Today's simplified 醜 has combined to 丑.

| |
|---|
| 甲骨文 |
| 金文 |
| 小篆 |
| 隶书 |
| 楷书 |
| 草书 |
| 行书 |
| 简化字 |

（同楷书）

48

# 臭 chòu, xiù

〔附〕嗅 xiù

The original meaning was "to smell by nose." Later, it was written as 嗅 and also a name for all the odors (the above items sounded xiù), especially "the terrible odor" (pronounced chòu). A dog's nose is the most sensible one, so 自 (鼻, nose) and 犬 (狗, dog) are joined together to constitute this character.

甲骨文

金文
（缺）

小篆

隶书

楷书

草书

行书

简化字
（同楷书）

49

# 处（處）chǔ, chù

From the unearthed objects of the Spring and Autumn and the Warring States Periods, the form of the character was a person leaning against 几 (jī, a small table) for a rest. The original meaning was 暂止, to pause or cease. In *Suo Wen*, 処 was regarded as an official version (similar to its simplified version), and its variant version was one of 虍 (sounded hū, tiger's head) to it.

| | |
|---|---|
| 甲骨文 | 𠇶 |
| 金文 | 𠇶 |
| 小篆 | 𥏡 |
| 隶书 | 處 |
| 楷书 | 處 |
| 草书 | 处 |
| 行书 | 處 |
| 简化字 | 处 |

# 穿 chuān

The original meaning is 穿透, to penetrate, 凿洞, to cut a hole. In bronze inscriptions, the lower part was 牙, tooth, referring to mice's tooth; the upper was 穴, cave. Mice are skilled in holing with their tip teeth.

| | |
|---|---|
| 甲骨文 | （缺） |
| 金文 | |
| 小篆 | |
| 隶书 | |
| 楷书 | 穿 |
| 草书 | |
| 行书 | |
| 简化字 | （同楷书） |

# 窗 chuāng

〔附〕囱 cōng

It was written as 囱 originally. Its variant version was 窗. The original meaning was "a skylight," and also referred to transom-windows of houses, vehicles and boats in a general sense.

（缺）

甲骨文

金文

小篆

隶书

楷书

草书

行书

（同楷书）

简化字

# 创（創剙）chuāng, chuàng

（缺）

Initially, it was "a self-explanatory character." On the edge of a knife were two strips of scars or two drops of blood. Subsequently, it developed itself into a phonogram, of which 刂（刀）indicated its meaning and 仓（倉）indicated its sound. The primitive significance was 创伤, trauma（pronounced chuāng）It is also loaned for use in 创造, creating（sounded chuàng）.

| | |
|---|---|
| 甲骨文 | 屮 |
| 金文 | 劊 |
| 小篆 | 創 |
| 隶书 | 剙 |
| 楷书 | 剏 |
| 草书 | |
| 行书 | |
| 简化字 | 创 |

# 床（牀）chuáng

〔附〕爿 pán

The original from was written as 爿, which is proved not only by the constitutions of 病 and 夢（the graphemes were often given vertically in oracle bone inscriptions when inventing characters）but also by the radicals of other characters, such as 將（将）and 牆（墙）.

| | |
|---|---|
| 甲骨文 | 爿 |
| 金文 | （缺） |
| 小篆 | 牀 |
| 隶书 | 牀 |
| 楷书 | 牀 |
| 草书 | 牀 |
| 行书 | 床 |
| 简化字 | 床 |

54

# 垂 chuí

〔附〕陲 chuí

In both oracle bone inscriptions and primitive seal characters, the grapheme was a plant with its leaves droopy on the ground. The original meaning was 下垂, droopy, 低下, low. The extended meaning was 流传, to hand down. In ancient books, it was interchangeable with 陲, borders.

# 刺 cì

It was originally written as 朿（not 束, shù）. In oracle bone and bronze inscriptions, the form of 朿 was a tree full of prickles. Since small seal characters, the radical 刂（刀）was added. Do not mistake it for 剌（là）.

（同楷书）

56

# 粗 CŪ

The original one was 麤. From oracle bone inscriptions to official script, it was constituted of two or three 鹿, deer. Later, it converted to indicate 不精, indelicacy, 粗劣, shoddy, 粗粮, coarse food grains, etc. In *Suo Wen*, it was also interpreted as 疏, sparse, distant, unfamiliar, etc.

甲骨文

金文

小篆

隶书

楷书

草书

行书

简化字

（同楷书）

# 毳 cuì

〔附〕脆 cuì 橇 qiāo

The original meaning was "fine hair of birds or beasts." With the constitution of three 毛, hair, the character indicated much fine hair. It was also interchangeable with 脆, fragile, and even 橇, sledge.

（缺）

甲骨文

金文

小篆

隶书

楷书

草书

行书

简化字

（同楷书）

58

寸 cùn

（缺）

甲骨文
金文
小篆
隶书
楷书
草书
行书
简化字

According to the traditional Chinese medicine, the wrist where a pulse can be felt by a hand is named 寸口, and the distance to palm is about one 寸, Chinese inch (about three centimeters). The graph of the character was made up of 又 (手) and 一 (a self-explanatory symbol), meaning the length of one 寸.

（同楷书）

# 逮 dài

The character was originally written as 隶 (dài, different from the simplified version of 隶 [lì, 隸]). The grapheme in bronze inscriptions was a hand having caught the tail of a beast. It primitively meant "to catch." In the later years, the radical 辵 (chuò i.e. 辶) was added to indicate the significance of action.

（缺）

（同楷书）

甲骨文

金文

小篆

隶书

楷书

草书

行书

简化字

# 弹 (彈) dàn, tán

It was the form of a slingshot in oracle bone inscriptions and on its string a metal pill. The initial meaning was 弹弓, slingshot, or also 弹丸, pill (pronounced dàn). In addition, it meant "to eject," "to knock at with fingers," " to play musical instrument," etc. (pronounced tán).

（缺）

彈

彈

彈

弹

弹

弹

# 道 dào

〔附〕导（導）dǎo

It was the original form of 导（導）. The outside is 行, meaning "road," and the middle is 首, meaning "to lead." The original meaning was "to guide." It also means "road."

（缺）

| 甲骨文 | （缺） |
| --- | --- |
| 金文 | 𦥑 |
| 小篆 | 䪫 |
| 隶书 | 道 |
| 楷书 | 道 |
| 草书 | 辶 |
| 行书 | 道 |
| 简化字 | （同楷书） |

# 到 dào

〔附〕倒 dǎo, dào

From the grapheme of bronze inscriptions, it should be composed of 至 and 人, referring to the coming of a man. Only in the later days, 人 turned to be 刀, which is understandable as a phonetic symbol though. It was interchangeable with 倒.

63

# 盗 dào

The upper part of the character was originally written as 次 (see character 涎), quite like a person who was drooling; the lower part was 皿, i.e. a container which was used to hold food. The original meaning is "to steal," and it also refers to "a person who has committed stealing," i.e. "thief."

(缺)

(同楷书)

甲骨文
金文
小篆
隶书
楷书
草书
行书
简化字

# 低 dī

〔附〕氐 dǐ 柢 dǐ 底 dǐ

At first it was 氐. Its graph was a man carrying a heavy thing with his body sideways, indicating "lowing." It was interchangeable with 柢, the tree's roots, and 底, bottom.

（同楷书）

65

# 翟 dí, Zhái

The original meaning was 野鸡, pheasant, and also named 雉, pheasant. The character is composed of 羽, feather, and 隹, showing that the feather of this kind of birds is very prominent. 墨子, Mo Zi, an ancient philosopher, was named 翟 dí. Today, as a surname it is pronounced Zhái.

甲骨文 （缺）

金文 翟

小篆 翟

隶书 翟

楷书 翟

草书 翟

行书 （同楷书）

简化字

66

# 弟 dì

〔附〕第 dì 悌 tì

The original significance was 次第 （次序，order）and it became 第 later on. Its graph was a stake（see character 弋）onto which some ropes were wound in a given order. Later, it was loaned for use in 兄弟 to mean brother. It was interchangeable with 悌, to respect and love elder brothers.

| 甲骨文 |
| 金文 |
| 小篆 |
| 隶书 |
| 楷书 |
| 草书 |
| 行书 |
| 简化字 |

（同楷书）

# 甸 diàn

〔附〕佃 diàn

In ancient writings，甸 and 佃 were the same one character. Its grapheme was a man laboring by the field；田，field，also signified sound. The original meaning was "to cultivate the field." The extended meanings were "to rent the field and to cultivate," "fields belonging to kings," "outskirts of a capital town," etc.

# 吊（弔）diào

〔附〕叔 shū 淑 shū

It was like a man holding a 隿 (yì, an arrow with a silk string). It was also the original form of 隿. The original meaning was no longer existed. In ancient books, it mostly meant 追悼死者, to mourn the dead，慰问，to express sympathy and solicitude for，伤悯，to grieve and sorrow，etc. In bronze inscriptions, it was interchangeable with 叔 in 叔伯 and also with 淑, virtuous.

| | |
|---|---|
| 甲骨文 | 𠂉 |
| 金文 | 𠂉 |
| 小篆 | 弔 |
| 隶书 | 吊 |
| 楷书 | 弔 |
| 草书 | 𠂉 |
| 行书 | （同楷书） |
| 简化字 | |

69

# 定 dìng

The upper part is 宀, meaning a house; the lower part is 正, meaning upright and foursquare. Only when the house is built foursquare, everything will be safe and peaceful. It also extends to signify 停息, to stop, 决定, to determine, 规定, to stipulate, 约定, to appoint, 必定, be bound to, etc.

（同楷书）

70

# 斗(鬥鬪)dòu

（缺）

The grapheme in oracle inscriptions was two warriors with feathers on their heads fighting furiously. The original meaning was 争斗, to contest, or 战斗, to fight. It was primitively written as 鬥, 鬪, etc. It used to have many variant forms which now have been simplified and combined to 斗.

71

# 短 duǎn

It is made of 矢 (an arrow, as a semantic symbol) and 豆 (a food container, as a phonetic symbol). In ancient times, the bow was long and the arrow short, hence the length of bow was borrowed as a unit to measure long objects and that of arrow to measure short ones. It extends to mean "short of," "scarce," "weak points," "slips," and so on.

甲骨文 （缺）

金文 （缺）

小篆 短

隶书 短

楷书 短

草书 短

行书 短

简化字 （同楷书）

# 段 duàn

〔附〕锻（鍛）duàn 碫 duàn 煅 duàn

The original form was 锻. In bronze inscriptions, it was a hand with a hammer beating a rock under the mountain cliff. The primitive meaning was 锤击, to strike with a hammer, or 锻炼, to forge and temple with fire. It was interchangeable with 碫 and 煅.

甲骨文 （缺）

金文 段

小篆 段

隶书 段

楷书 段

草书 耖

行书 段

简化字 （同楷书）

73

# 堆 duī

It was 自 originally. The earliest form looked a bit like two mounds (in oracle bone inscriptions, the characters of horizontal-width were usually given in a vertical structure, such as 阜，犬，豕，etc.) However, 堆 evolved into a new phonogram later on.

金文

小篆

隶书

楷书

草书

行书

简化字

（同楷书）

# 敦 dūn

It was a name for a meal utensil in the primitive time and pronounced duì. Hence, the form in bronze inscriptions was like a hand with a spoon putting the mutton into a meal utensil. In ancient books, it was usually used to mean 质朴, simplicity, 厚实, candid, 勤勉, intelligent, 督促, supervise and urge, and so on.

甲骨文

金文

小篆

隶书

楷书

草书

行书

简化字

（同楷书）

75

# 夺（奪）duó

A hand caught a bird and then hid it in the clothes, so it was easy to lose it again. The initial meaning was 失漏, to lose or leak. As 夺 in 争夺, fighting to gain something, its orthodox form was written as 敓, whose significance was expressed later by 夺 as a loan word. As a result, 敓 has been out of use.

（缺）

# 娥 é

A phonogram: of which 女 indicated meaning and 我 indicated sound. It originally meant 美好, fine. It also referred to 美女, beautiful woman.

（缺）

（同楷书）

# 厄 è

〔附〕轭（軛）è

厄 was the original form of 轭（軛，軛）. Graphically in bronze inscriptions, it looked like a gear round the neck of a horse or an ox for pulling the cart. In the later years, it mostly meant 险隘, a narrow pass, 困苦, hardship, 灾难, disaster, etc.

甲骨文

（缺）

金文

小篆

隶书

楷书

草书

行书

简化字

（同楷书）

# 而 ér

The graph of the character was like the beard drooping from one's cheeks. Its initial meaning was no longer existent later on. It was often used as a conjunction or a pronoun (referring to the 2nd person), hence another character 耏 was invented to express the initial significance.

甲骨文

金文

小篆

隶书

楷书

草书

行书

简化字

（同楷书）

79

# 二 èr

Two numbering chips（in ancient
times, bamboo chips were used for num-
bering）are placed in a parallel structure, signifying the numeral two（二）. It
extends to indicate 两样, different, and
不专一, not being emotionally attached
to one, 不忠诚, disloyal to. The variant
forms are 弍,贰 and others.

（同楷书）

# 发（發髮）fā, fà

A man running fast and casting a javelin was its graph in oracle bone inscriptions. But since bronze inscriptions, the radical 弓 was added to its forms. The initial meaning was 发射, to eject. The simplified version originated from grass stroke characters, and has combined 髮 into 发.

# 罚（罰）fá

It is made up of three forms: 网, 言 and 刀, signifying "the arm of law" (i. e. law), "to sentence or verdict," and "to punish with a torture instrument." Its initial meaning was 过错, error. The extended meanings are "to fine," "to punish," or even "to atone for one's crime with payment."

甲骨文 （缺）

金文

小篆

隶书

楷书

草书

行书

简化字

82

乏 fá

The original meaning was 不正, slanting. It usually took on the meanings of 缺少, short of, 匮乏, scarce, in ancient books.

（缺）

区

乑

乏

乏

乏

（同楷书）

甲骨文

金文

小篆

隶书

楷书

草书

行书

简化字

# 法 fǎ

It was written as 灋 initially. It was said in *Suo Wen* that in ancient times a godly animal named 解（獬）廌（xièzhì）, whose shape was like an ox but with only one horn or antler, could judge who was not right and then "headed him away" （去, abandon）. Hence, the animal was used to settle a lawsuit. The law case must be executed equally, so the radical 水 was added. Subsequently, it is simplified to be 法.

（缺）

（同楷书）

甲骨文

金文

小篆

隶书

楷书

草书

行书

简化字

84

# 番 fān, pān

〔附〕蹯 fán

It was initially written as 釆 ( not 采 ), whose shape was like an animal's sole. Beasts usually leave their footprints in the field, so the radical 田 was added to the forms of the character later. After that, 番 was mostly loaned to convey some other ideas, therefore another character 蹯 ( today pronounced fán ) was originated.

| 甲骨文 | 金文 | 小篆 | 隶书 | 楷书 | 草书 | 行书 | 简化字 |
|---|---|---|---|---|---|---|---|

（同楷书）

# 繁 fán

It was the original form of 緐. The left part is a woman (每) and the right is a bundle of silk. In order to make silk a great numbers of thin silk were needed, hence the original meaning was 多, many. Later, it was written as 繁.

（缺）

甲骨文

金文

小篆

隶书

楷书

草书

行书

简化字

（同楷书）

86

# 樊 fán

〔附〕藩 fān

A pair of hands is weaving fences with tree trunks and tree branches or something. The primitive meaning was endowed with 篱笆, fences. But in bronze inscriptions, the middle became a graph of cross. Since small seal characters, it has been added two cross forms. It is also written as 藩 to give the same meaning.

（缺）

（同楷书）

87

# 犯 fàn

The earliest character was discovered in the scripts of the Warring States Period. The left part was a dog and the right a kneeling man. The initial meaning was 侵犯, to attack or infringe. It extends to mean 抵触, conflict, 冒犯, offense, 犯罪, commit a crime, 犯人, prisoner, etc.

（缺）

甲骨文

战国文字

小篆

隶书

楷书

草书

行书

简化字

（同楷书）

# 妃 fēi

It was made of 女 and 己 (as a phonetic symbol) initially and took on the meaning of 匹, a spouse. Later, it exclusively referred to wife or wives of emperors, kings, princes, and marquises.

甲骨文

金文

小篆

隶书

楷书

草书

行书

简化字

(同楷书)

# 匪 fěi

〔附〕筐 fěi 非 fēi

It is the initial form of 筐, which was a bamboo container like a basket. 匪 was made up of 匸, and 非 (as a phonetic symbol), of which 匸 (fāng) was a square container. Subsequently, it was loaned for use in 匪徒 to mean "bandit." It was also interchangeable with 非 in ancient books.

（缺）

甲骨文

金文

小篆

隶书

楷书

草书

行书

简化字

（同楷书）

# 吠 fèi

It had appeared in oracle bone inscriptions. However, it was not found in bronze inscriptions but in ancient seal characters of the pre-Qin days. This is an associate compound character, composing of 犬 and 口, and referring to dog's barking.

| |
|---|
| 甲骨文 |
| 古玺文 |
| 小篆 |
| 隶书 |
| 楷书 |
| 草书 |
| 行书 |
| 简化字 |

（同楷书）

91

# 焚 fén

It is an associate compound character. It obviously takes on the meaning of
烧, burning, for a big fire has already
caused a terrible burning in the forest. In
ancient times, people usually burnt the
forest in order to grow crops or hunt animals.

小篆

隶书

楷书

草书

行书

简化字

（同楷书）

# 奋（奮）fèn

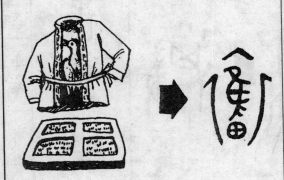

A man caught a bird and hid it in his clothes, and the bird was struggling to fly into the field. It originally meant "a bird soaring into the sky with its spreading wings." Later, it extended to mean 振作, pull up one's slacks, 奋发, stir oneself, 举起, raise up, etc.

（缺）

| | |
|---|---|
| 甲骨文 | （缺） |
| 金文 | 奮 |
| 小篆 | 奮 |
| 隶书 | 奮 |
| 楷书 | 奮 |
| 草书 | 奮 |
| 行书 | 奮 |
| 简化字 | 奋 |

93

# 粪（糞）fèn

The grapheme in oracle bone inscriptions was one hand with a broom and another with a dustpan throwing away the dirty things. It meant 扫除, to give a cleaning, primitively. Subsequently, it began to signify 粪便, dung. The form of the character has been altered a great deal and it is difficult to understand its significance and its origins.

# 封 fēng

A hand banking up a newly planted tree with earth was the graph in both oracle bone and bronze inscriptions. The primitive people marked the border just by such a way of planting trees. Hence, it has the meaning of 疆界, boundary.

甲骨文·

金文

小篆

隶书

楷书

草书

行书

简化字

封

封

封

封

封

封

（同楷书）

# 奉 fèng

〔附〕捧 pěng

This was the original form of 捧. Graphically it looks like a hand holding a budding tree or grass. Later, 奉 is mostly endowed with the significance of respect. Its extended meanings are "to receive," "to respect," "to believe in," "to serve."

（同楷书）

96

# 肤（膚）fū

It refers to human body's skin. The character was made up of 月 (i.e. 肉, indicating meaning) and 盧 (of which 皿 was moved in bronze inscriptions, indicating sound). In small seal characters, it was written 臚. The grapheme in official script inherited that of bronze inscriptions rather than of small seal characters. The simplified character has taken 夫 as its phonetic symbol to originate a new pictophonetic one：肤.

97

# 伏 fú

A dog stooped down behind a man and wanted to attack him any time. The original meaning was "to attack for one's chance." It again contains the meanings of 俯伏, proneness, 藏匿, hiding, 屈服, giving up, etc. It means "to low," in the idiom of 此起彼伏, one falls and another rises.

98

# 扶 fú

Graphically in oracle bone inscriptions, it was a strong man stretching his hand to support another. Since bronze inscriptions, it has become a big hand supporting a man（夫 also signifying sound）. The original meaning was 帮助, to help, 搀扶, to support by hand.

甲骨文
金文
小篆
隶书
楷书
草书
行书
简化字

（同楷书）

# 凫 （鳬） fú

The original meaning was 野鸭, wild duck. The character was constituted of 鸟, bird, indicating meaning and 勹, indicating sound.

（缺）

# 府 fǔ

〔附〕腑 fǔ

It originally meant "a place where written documents or properties were stored." In bronze inscriptions, it was formed by 宀, 贝, and 付 (as a phonetic symbol); since small seal characters, it came to consist of 广 and 付 as a sound symbol. It extends to mean 官府, local authorities, 乐府, the music office in Han Dynasty and their collected folk poems and music, 学府, institute of higher learning, 行政区划名称, a name for regionalism, and 达官贵人的住宅, houses of high officials and nobles. In addition, it has got a meaning of 腑脏, heart, and later as 腑.

（缺）

甲骨文

金文

小篆

隶书

楷书

草书

行书

简化字

（同楷书）

# 釜 fǔ

釜 was a cooking utensil in ancient times. In bronze inscriptions, most versions were constituted of 缶 (indicating meaning), and 父 (indicating sound). The orthodox version of small seal characters was written as 鬴, and the unorthodox was one of 金 and 夫 (as a phonetic symbol). The first two strokes in regular script were simplified, such as 铁，铗，钻，锥，釜,镘 and 鍫.

富 fù

In a house is a wine vessel and it symbolizes a rich life, of which 畐 also represented sound. It means "many" or "much". Later, it mostly refers to "wealth," "much property."

甲骨文

（缺）

金文

小篆

隶书

楷书

草书

行书

（同楷书）

简化字

# 阜 fù

The original meaning was "earth hills." The initial grapheme was like the shape of "hills" but in a vertical structure (such a case was popular with oracle bone inscriptions). When using as a radical in regular script, it was as 阝 (on the left).

（同楷书）

104

# 付 fù

A hand is delivering something to another. The graph of hand（手）in bronze inscriptions was mostly written 又, and in small seal characters was 寸. The character's meaning is "to give."

（同楷书）

105

# 敢 gǎn

A big hand caught a violent beast, which is certainly a very brave act. The lower left part of the character is 甘 (gān), signifying its sound. It means "brave."

（同楷书）

106

# 刚（剛）gāng

〔附〕钢（鋼）gāng

Composed of 刀, knife, and 网, net, it was an associate compound character. Its original meaning was 尖利, sharp, for a knife could cut a net. It extends to indicate 坚硬, hardship, 强劲, strong, against 柔 in meaning. It was interchangeable with 钢（鋼）, steel.

甲骨文

金文

小篆

隶书

楷书

草书

行书

简化字

107

杲 gǎo

The sun has already risen over the top of trees, indicating the brightest time in the sky. Its initial meaning is "bright." See character 杳, pronounced yǎo.

（同楷书）

108

# 革 gé

金文

小篆

隶书

楷书

草书

行书

简化字

（同楷书）

Its initial meaning is "the animal's leather after the fur being processed and the hair wiped off." In bronze inscriptions, its grapheme was like a fine-processed animal's leather including the parts of head and tail, among which the middle wide part indicates the leather and the two dots are only self-explanatory symbols. It extends to mean 更改, change, 除去, remove, etc.

109

# 肱 gōng

It was the original form of 厷. In o-racle bone inscriptions, its grapheme was like a small arc added on the elbow, meaning mussels. It originally meant "arm." Its form didn't change in bronze inscriptions. However, 肱, with the added radical of 月（肉）, was considered a variant form.

（同楷书）

甲骨文

古玺文

小篆

隶书

楷书

草书

行书

简化字

110

# 巩（鞏）gǒng

（缺）

甲骨文
金文
小篆
隶书
楷书
草书
行书
简化字

Originally 巩 was written as 鞏. In bronze inscriptions, the character was like a kneeling man raising two hands and holding tools. The radical 工 also signifies sound. Its initial meaning was "to raise" or "to hold and carry." In small seal characters, 革 was added to denote to bind with the leather ropes, meaning 巩固, consolidate.

111

# 骨 gǔ

In oracle bone inscriptions, graphically it was a few bones interlocked there one another, of which the short vertical strokes represented the two protruding ends of the joint. Later, the radical 月（肉）has been added to denote "linking of bone and flesh." In regular script, the previous version was written as 骨 and its new form is as 骨 for its writing convenience.

| | |
|---|---|
| 甲骨文 | ㄥ |
| 古璽文 | 骨 |
| 小篆 | 骨 |
| 隶书 | 骨 |
| 楷书 | 骨 |
| 草书 | 骨 |
| 行书 | 骨 |
| 简化字 | （同楷书） |

112

# 古 gǔ

〔附〕故 gù

The upper part is like a shield（盾）indicating wars; the lower a mouth（口）indicating to narrate. Together it means to relate the warfare stories in the past. The character originally meant 古代，ancient times. It was interchangeable with 故，old or former.

| | |
|---|---|
| 甲骨文 | |
| 金文 | |
| 小篆 | |
| 隶书 | |
| 楷书 | |
| 草书 | |
| 行书 | |
| （同楷书） | 简化字 |

113

# 蛊（蠱）gǔ

It was a kind of poisonous worm （虫）cultivated man-made to harm or hurt others in ancient times. The graph in oracle bone inscriptions was a 皿 (a container) with one or two worms inside, subsequently three, and today's simplified character has again returned to one worm.

# 瓜 guā

（缺）

甲骨文

金文

小篆

隶书

楷书

草书

行书

简化字

In bronze inscriptions it was a vivid delineation that out of the liana was growing an oval melon. However, since the time of official script, the character changed to be little pictographic. It extended to indicate "the melon being ripe."

（同楷书）

115

寡 guǎ

In a house, an old woman was living lonely with sorrows in her eyes. The primitive meaning of 寡 was "one who lost wife or husband," in general or exclusively "one who lost husband when aged." Emperors and kings in ancient times often modestly address themselves as 寡人, meaning "a less moral person."

（缺）

（同楷书）

# 官 guān

〔附〕馆(舘)guǎn

With a construction built highly on the earth hill（自, see character 堆）, its original meaning was "a house for officials to live or stay." Hence, it was also the primitive form of 馆, a guest house. Later, it extended to indicate 官职, official position，官吏，officials，and other meanings with the association of 官府, local authorities.

（同楷书）

117

# 关（關）guān

It was not discovered in oracle bone inscriptions, but in bronze inscriptions, the character took the shape of two doors between which two wooden sticks and a ring-shaped lock was placed. The original meaning was "a lock," or "a latch." Later, it extended to mean 关闭, to close，要塞, fort.

118

# 冠 guān, guàn

The character is made up of three parts: 宀, indicating a cap, 元, man's head (see character 元), 寸, the same as 又, a hand. Three parts together signify to put a cap on one's head with hand. The earliest meaning was 帽子, a cap (pronounced guān); when meaning "to put up a cap," sounded guàn.

（缺）

（缺）

甲骨文

金文

小篆

隶书

楷书

草书

行书

简化字

（同楷书）

119

# 贯（貫）guàn

〔附〕惯（慣）guàn

The earliest grapheme was with something stick-shaped or rope-shaped to thread one object or two. The primitive meaning was "to thread." In ancient times, 贝, cowrie, was regarded as a kind of currency, hence, the radical 贝 was added. Since it was loaned to indicate 习惯, habit, it was written 惯. The upper part shouldn't be mistaken for 母 or 毋.

120

# 广（廣）guǎng

〔附〕旷（曠）kuàng

In oracle bone inscriptions, it originally constituted 宀 (the graph of a house) and 黄, yellow, as a phonetic symbol. Its initial significance was "a large house with no walls around. Since bronze inscriptions, the radical turned out to be 厂 or 广. The extended meaning is 大, big, or 宽阔, wide and broad. It also extends to mean 推广, spread, 众多, numerous, 广泛, far and wide, etc. It was interchangeable with 旷, vast or spacious.

# 归（歸）guī

The original meaning was "a girl who is getting married." It is composed of 帚, broom, and 𠂤: 帚 is the simplified version of 妇, which was the common form in oracle bone inscriptions; 𠂤 is the original form of 堆, "heap," signifying sound. In the later years, it extends to mean 返回, return, 归还, give back, etc.

寒 hán

A man with his barefoot was standing on two pieces of ice blocks in a house (see character 冰), hence meaning it was very cold. Although he placed some hay around to warm himself, it couldn't help to endure the coldness. In *Suo Wen*, the explanation was "freezing."

甲骨文 （缺）

金文

小篆 寒

隶书 寒

楷书 寒

草书 寒

行书 寒

简化字 （同楷书）

123

# 河 hé

It initially referred to the Yellow River, a proper term. Later, it became a general term for all the rivers. Its phonetic radical differed in different versions: in oracle bone inscriptions, 丂 (see character 可); in bronze inscriptions, 何; since small seal characters, 可.

甲骨文

金文

小篆

隶书

楷书

草书

行书

简化字

（同楷书）

# 盍 hé

〔附〕盖（蓋）gài

The original form of the character was 盖（蓋）, meaning 覆, to cover, or to overturn. It was interchangeable with 蓋. In ancient writings, 盍 was often used as a pronoun to mean 何, why; also as an adverb to indicate 何不, why not.

（缺）

盒
盍
盍
盍
盍
盍

（同楷书）

# 赫 hè

〔附〕吓（嚇）xià

The character is composed of two 赤. Since 赤 is loaned to indicate "red color" with 大 and 火; hence, reasonably 赫 will take on the meaning of "bright red color." In addition, it is endowed with a significance of 显耀, conspicuous or staring. It was interchangeable with 嚇（吓）.

# 黑 hēi

From the objects and articles unearthed from the Yin ruins, the character 黑 is an associate compound: the lower part is a burning hearth (灶台); the upper part is a chimney with a square mouth; the middle dots signify the flying dusts. The original meaning was "the color smoked by the fire, i.e. black color."

| | |
|---|---|
| （缺） | 甲骨文 |
| 黑 | 金文 |
| 黑 | 小篆 |
| 黑 | 隶书 |
| 黑 | 楷书 |
| 黑 | 草书 |
| 黑 | 行书 |
| （同楷书） | 简化字 |

# 恒 héng

〔附〕亘 gèn

In oracle bone inscriptions, the character was not formed by the radical 心, of which the upper and the lower planes represented the sky and the earth respectively, and the middle is a crescent. It initially meant "the first quarter moon turning into a full one." Since bronze inscriptions, the radical 心 has been added to indicate "long," "usually," "insistent," etc.

甲骨文

金文

小篆

隶书

楷书

草书

行书

简化字

（同楷书）

# 宏 hóng

In bronze inscriptions, the character didn't have the radical 宀 but similar to that of 函. From its grapheme, it must be a leather bag for storing bows. After small seal characters, the radical 宀 was added. With the primitive meanings not existent, it was usually loaned to mean 广大, immensity, 宽博, wide and profound, 发扬, foster or develop, etc. in ancient books.

| | |
|---|---|
| 甲骨文 | （缺） |
| 金文 | |
| 小篆 | |
| 隶书 | 宏 |
| 楷书 | 宏 |
| 草书 | 宏 |
| 行书 | 宏 |
| 简化字 | （同楷书） |

# 厚 hòu

Under the cliff（山崖，graph of 厂）
was placed a container with big mouth
and small body, which might be made by
stones so it looked very thick and heavy.
Its variant form in ancient times was written as 垕, and came out of use later.

甲骨文

金文

小篆

隶书

楷书

草书

行书

简化字

（同楷书）

130

# 乎 hū

The character's lower part is 丂
(the original form of 柯, an ax handle)
indicating sound; the upper is three short
vertical strokes indicating the rising of
the sound. It differed slightly from 兮
(see character 兮). Mostly, it was used
as a form of expression in ancient writings.

# 互 hù

〔附〕笂 hù

It was the original form of 笂, meaning "a device to draw in ropes." Graphically, it looked like a bamboo utensil with a thin axis in the center. It is often loaned to mean 交错, interweave，彼此, one another, and so on.

（缺）

互

笂

互

互

互

互

（同楷书）

132

# 华（華）huá

〔附〕花 huā

It was the initial form of 花, flowers. A flower in blossom was the graph in bronze inscriptions. Since small seal characters it has began to add ⺿ (草字头) as a radical. Its extended meanings are "splendor," "brilliancy," "prosperity," and so on.

133

# 怀（懷）huái

It was written as 褱 originally. Composed of 衣 and 罞 (the ancient form of 涕）, it indicated "the emotion deeply hidden in one's heart bottom which will cause someone to weep for such a miss, i.e. 怀念, "to miss." It also means 怀藏, conceal in mind.

（缺）

甲骨文

金文

小篆

隶书

楷书

草书

行书

简化字

134

# 环（環）huán

Written originally as 瞏, the character was constituted of ⺫ (eyes), 衣, clothes, and ○ (a circular jade article), meaning a man gazing and admiring a ring（环）in his chest with his eyes widely open.

135

# 宦 huàn

The character originally meant "to be a slave or a servant of feudal nobles," with its constitution of 宀 (the form of house) and 臣 (slave). Later, it extended to mean 宦官, eunuch, etc.

金文

小篆

隶书

楷书

草书

行书

简化字

（同楷书）

# 幻 huàn

It meant "to cheat" originally. In small seal characters, the graph of 幻 was the reflection of 予 (see character 予) in the mirror: 予 is 给予, to give, hence 幻 is "to cheat" or "nothingness."

（同楷书）

# 豢 huàn

Two hands caught a wild boar and had it raised in the pen. According to *Suo Wen*, the meaning of 豢 was "to raise pigs with grains in a pen." It also generally refers to "raising livestock."

甲骨文

（缺）

金文

小篆

隶书

楷书

草书

行书

简化字

（同楷书）

138

# 皇 huáng

〔附〕煌 huáng

皇 was the initial form of 煌, in which its lower part was originally a lamp holder, and its upper part was three vertical strokes representing the lamp light. In small seal characters, the upper part changed to 自, and then to 白 in official script, quite incomprehensible. Its extended meanings are 大, big, 帝王, emperors and kings, etc.

（缺）

甲骨文

金文

皇
皇
皇
皂
皇

小篆

隶书

楷书

草书

行书

（同楷书）

简化字

139

# 惠 huì

惠
慧
惠
惠
垂
惠

（同楷书）

This is a phonogram: whose graphic radical is 心 (the meaning symbol); whose phonetic radical is 叀 (the sound symbol, spindles in ancient times). The primitive meaning of the character is 仁, benevolence. Sometimes it was interchangeable with 慧, intelligent.

# 彗 huì

甲骨文

说文『古文』

小篆

隶书

楷书

草书

行书

简化字

In *Suo Wen*, the explanation of its significance was a bamboo broom. In small seal characters, the grapheme was a hand taking two bamboo brooms. The word 彗星（comets）was firstly appeared two thousands years ago in a book named *Er Ya*, for its shape quite like a broom.

（同楷书）

141

# 慧 huì

It is a phonogram, composed of 心 as a graphic radical（meaning symbol）and 彗 as a phonetic radical（sound symbol, see character 彗）. The original meaning is 聪明, intelligent or 智慧, wisdom. As a Buddhism term, it means 了悟, "completely aware of." In traditional Chinese medicine, it refers to "clear and bright eyes."

（同楷书）

142

# 卉 huì

It referred to a general term for all the grass. Its grapheme is just three pieces of grass, representing a multitude of grass (many cases in ancient characters so as to invent new ones by using "a few" to replace "many," such as 品, 森, 多, and others). Later, it commonly refers to 草木, grass and trees, and also 花, flowers.

# 祸（禍）huò

The character's significance was represented by the bone pieces of beasts. Since bronze inscriptions, the radicals 示 and 口, were both added as its meaning symbol. The earliest meaning was 害, disaster or catastrophe.

144

# 几₁ jī, jǐ

（缺）

金文

小篆

隶书

楷书

草书

行书

简化字

Its form before small seal characters can only be found in the character of 处 （see character 处）which was unearthed with the other objects of the Spring and Autumn and the Warring States Periods. 几 was a kind of small table in ancient times. Today，茶几 is still in use. In simplified characters 幾 has been combined to 几.

（同楷书）

# 几₂（幾）jī, jǐ

〔附〕机（機）jī

It was made up of 丝 (yōu, puniness) and 戍 (shù, to guard). The weak defense power is really a dangerous thing, so the original meaning was "danger," "crisis." In addition, it has a meaning of 细微, slight, or fine. Sometimes it was interchangeable with 機 (机). The simplified version of 幾 has been combined to 几.

146

基 jī

甲骨文
金文
小篆
隶书
楷书
草书
行书
简化字

（同楷书）

The original meaning is "the foundation of a construction." The character is composed of 土（indicating meaning）and 其（the original form of 箕, indicating sound）. It extends to mean "the essence or the foundation of things or matters." It also has the meanings of 起头, start or at first, and 开始, begin.

147

# 姬 jī

甲骨文
金文
小篆
隶书
楷书
草书
行书
简化字

（同楷书）

The character constitutes 女 and 匝 （jī, not 臣）, the former indicates meaning and the latter is 笸 （jī, a comb with thin and dense teeth） indicating sound. In the legend it was said that Huang Di's family name was 姬, and again it is a good name for women. In ancient writings, it was used as 歌女, singing and dancing girls, and 妾, concubines.

148

# 亟 jí, qì

〔附〕极（極）jí

It was the primitive character of 极.
In oracle bone inscriptions, it was graphically a man standing on the earth and his
head touching the sky, indicating "limit," or "apex." When indicating 急速,
fast speed，赶快, hurry up, it is pronounced jí; it is sounded qì when meaning 屡次, frequent, and 一再, over and
over again.

甲骨文

金文

小篆

隶书

楷书

草书

行书

简化字

（同楷书）

149

急 jí

急 + ♥

➡ 急

It was originally made up of 心 and 及 as a sound symbol. But its phonetic radical, since *li bian*, the change of official script, has been difficult to trace back to. Its original meaning is 心急, impatience or short-tempered. Its extended meanings are 急速, at high speed, 急躁, hot-tempered, 紧急, emergency, 窘迫, embarrassment, 急需, urgent need, etc.

150

# 棘 jí

It is the name for a plant, i.e. "wild jujube," and also a general term for all the thorny plants, e.g. 荆棘, brambles. The character is constituted of two juxtaposed 朿 (cì, 刺; if a "upper and low" structure, it is 枣 [棗]). The character in official script was erroneously formed by two 束 (shù).

（缺）

棘

棘

棘

棘

棘

（同楷书）

甲骨文

金文

小篆

隶书

楷书

草书

行书

简化字

# 己 jǐ

〔附〕纪（紀）jì

It was the original form of 纪. The ancient people kept a record of events by tying knots. Its grapheme was just like a rope neatly placed. Afterwards, the character was loaned to indicate one of the ten Heavenly Stems and function as a pronoun.

| | |
|---|---|
| 甲骨文 | 己 |
| 金文 | 己 |
| 小篆 | 己 |
| 隶书 | 己 |
| 楷书 | 己 |
| 草书 | 己 |
| 行书 | 己 |
| 简化字 | （同楷书） |

# 戟 jǐ

It was the name for an ancient weapon, long shaft, straight blade on the top end, horizontal blade on both sides, which can stab straight, attack sideways or backwards. For it was a powerful weapon, it had the radical of 肉.

（缺）

戓

戟

戟

戟

戟

（同楷书）

| 甲骨文 |
|---|
| 金文 |
| 小篆 |
| 隶书 |
| 楷书 |
| 草书 |
| 行书 |
| 简化字 |

# 继（繼）jì

It meant "continuous" originally. The grapheme in bronze inscriptions was like two binds of silk half cut or half linked. After small seal characters, the radical 糸 was added to its forms. It extends to mean 继承, inherit, 随后, afterwards, 接济, give financial help to, 增益, increase profits, etc.

甲骨文

金文

小篆

隶书

楷书

草书

行书

简化字

154

# 季 jì

〔附〕稚 zhì

It is the original form of 稚 (穉). The original meaning was "seedlings." With the constitution of 禾 and 子, it indicates the infantile crops. It extends to signify "juniors."

| | |
|---|---|
| | 甲骨文 |
| | 金文 |
| | 小篆 |
| | 隶书 |
| | 楷书 |
| | 草书 |
| | 行书 |
| | 简化字 |

（同楷书）

155

# 加 jiā

The original meaning was "to praise," "to honor." Later, the character was often loaned for use in other items, hence another character 嘉 was coined. The form of bronze inscriptions was made up of 力（耒, ploughing instrument）and 口, indicating that diligent labors are always complimented all the time.

（缺）

金文

小篆

隶书

楷书

草书

行书

简化字

（同楷书）

156

# 嘉 jiā

嘉 was written as 加 originally and it meant "to praise," "to honor." This character was constituted by placing 壴 (i.e. 鼓, drum) onto the top of character 加, hence its jubilant atmosphere was more obvious. It also takes on the meanings of "beauty and virtue," "prosperous," "happy," etc.

157

# 假 jiǎ, jià

It was primitively written as 叚 and meant "to loan." In bronze inscriptions, it was vividly depicted that two hands（representing two persons）exchanged goods one another under the mountain cliff.

（缺）

叚

假

假

俉

假

（同楷书）

甲骨文

金文

小篆

隶书

楷书

草书

行书

简化字

158

# 肩 jiān

The original meaning was "the body between neck and arm." The upper part 户 has nothing to do with doors here but an indication of the shoulder graph, and the lower part 月 meant flesh. It extends to indicate "to shoulder," "qualified for," "appoint," etc.

（同楷书）

159

# 兼 jiān

Just compare a difference between holding a handful of plants and holding two handfuls of plants: the former is 秉 and the latter is 兼. The original meaning is "to have or concern several things or objects at the same time."

# 柬 jiǎn

〔附〕拣（揀）jiǎn 简（簡）jiǎn

It was the original form of 拣（揀），indicating "to choose," "to select." It is composed of 束（a cloth bag）and 八（to divide）and means "to take out the things from the bag and put them into different categories." In addition, it was interchangeable with 简.

161

# 间（間）jiàn, jiān

By 门 and 月 was the character constituted. For it is a self-explanatory one, it signifies that the moon could be seen through the narrow opening of two shutters of the door or gate. The initial meaning was "narrow opening," or "slit." Later, it was exchangeable in usage with 闲（閒, see character 闲）in 空闲, hence another character 间 was invented.

（缺）

甲骨文

金文

小篆

隶书

楷书

草书

行书

简化字

# 建 jiàn

〔附〕健 jiàn

（缺）

甲骨文
金文
小篆
隶书
楷书
草书
行书
简化字

In *Suo Wen*, the explanation of 建 was "to set up the court administration laws and decrees." 聿, i.e. 笔, represents the law in here; 彳 and 止 both indicated "action," which later turned into the radical of 廴. It extends to signify "to set up," "to establish," "to construct," etc. It was interchangeable with 健.

（同楷书）

163

# 荐（薦）jiàn

It was 薦 originally. The initial meaning was "the edible grass for beasts." In bronze inscriptions, the character resembled an animal, *xie zhi* (解［獬］廌), a godly beast in the legend) with some grass around. It extended to mean "a grass mat." The simplified character of 荐 already appeared in small seal characters and these two ones were exchangeable in early time.

（缺）

# 江 jiāng

Firstly it referred to the Yangtse River, a proper term. Later, it began to indicate all the large long rivers. It was made up of 水 (a graphic radical) and 工 (a phonetic radical).

（缺）

（同楷书）

165

# 姜 (薑) jiāng

The ancient tribes often adored totems, so some family names originated from totems and had the radical of 女 for there had been the matrilineal society before. 姜 was said to be a surname of 神农氏 (the Holy Farmer, a legendary ruler, the 2nd of the three August Ones, supposed to have invented the plough and discovered the curative virtues of plants), of which 羊, goat, was regarded as a totem. Today, the simplified character has also replaced 薑.

| | |
|---|---|
| 甲骨文 | 𦍒 |
| 金文 | 𦍒 |
| 小篆 | 𦍒 |
| 隶书 | 姜 |
| 楷书 | 姜 |
| 草书 | 姜 |
| 行书 | 姜 |
| 简化字 | (同楷书) |

166

# 缰（繮）jiāng

The initial meaning was "the ropes to tie livestock." Graphically in oracle bone inscriptions, it resembled a hand pulling the rein; since bronze inscriptions it has altered to be a phonogram: of which 糸 indicates meaning and 畺 indicates sound.

（缺）

# 匠 jiàng

This is an associate compound character. The exterior frame 匚 (fāng) is a square container and 斤 is an ax. A person going to work with an ax is called a carpenter.

（缺）

（同楷书）

# 焦 jiāo

A big fire was burning one（but in small seal characters were three）bird（隹，zhuī）. The initial meaning was 烧伤, to burn（an injury）. In addition, another meaning was "to burn dark by fire," in *Yu Pian*, an ancient book on Chinese characters.

（同楷书）

169

# 皆 jiē

〔附〕偕 xié

It was primitively composed of two 人, person（indicating many）and 曰（indicating saying or speaking）. The initial meaning was 都, indicating that everybody gave the same saying. It also took on the significance of 同, and written as 偕 later on.

甲骨文（缺）

金文

小篆

隶书

楷书

草书

行书

简化字（同楷书）

# 节 （節）jié

Its earliest form was given as 卩. In oracle bone inscriptions, its graph looked like a man in a kneeling position and with his knee joints popped out. Later, it was loaned for use in 符节 (also as 瑞信, a pass or certificate to prove one's identification). After that, the radical 竹 was added to express "bamboo joints." The extended meanings are "abstinence," "moral integrity," "etiquette," "season," "festival," etc.

甲骨文

金文

小篆

隶书

楷书

草书

行书

简化字

# 今 jīn

〔附〕含 hán

It was the earliest form of 含, of which the upper part is a reversal 口, and the lower plane indicates something kept in the mouth. This can be proved by the inscriptions on Zhong Shan King Tripod（中山王鼎）that 今 was written as 含. With the time going, the original meaning was gone and it is loaned to mean 是时也, at the present time or period.

甲骨文

金文

小篆

隶书

楷书

草书

行书

简化字

（同楷书）

172

# 金 jīn

The character 金 is "the common term for all metals." It was not discovered in oracle bone inscriptions. In early bronze inscriptions, it resembled two metal ingots; later a crucible (坩埚, gānguō) form was added to its side to indicate melting metals. Since then, it only referred to gold. Today, 金属, metal, 五金, the five metals (gold, silver, copper, iron, and tin), etc. still refer to many metals.

甲骨文　（缺）

金文　二

小篆　金

隶书　金

楷书　金

草书　金

行书　金

简化字　（同楷书）

# 尽（盡 儘）jìn, jǐn

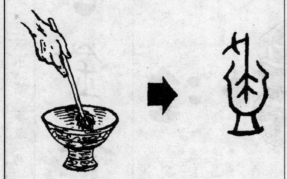

A hand is taking a kitchen broom washing dinner utensils（皿），meaning the eating-out. The original meaning was 竭, exhaust，完, finish. The extended meanings are 达到极限, to reach the limit，终, to end，死, to die, and others. The simplified characters have combined 盡 and 儘 to 尽.

# 经（經）jīng

The initial meaning is "warps, the vertical threads on the loom" (the horizontal threads are wefts). It was initially written as 坙. Three vertical curve treads signify warps; with 一 and 工 put together the brief shape of a loom is given. Since small seal characters, the radical 糸 has been added to indicate meaning.

175

兢 jīng

金文

小篆

隶书

楷书

草书

行书

简化字

（同楷书）

In bronze inscriptions, graphically it was like two persons with heavy things on their heads and seeming to be very cautious and on the jig. Its initial meaning was "careful and prudent." It also has the meaning of 坚强, strong.

176

# 荆 jīng

金文

小篆

隶书

楷书

草书

行书

简化字

（同楷书）

A name for shrub plants. With its great variety, their branches can be used to weave baskets. Its graph resembles a piece of shrub and on its tender branch was X-shape（and some,｜-shape）as self-explanatory symbols to indicate that this is a usable part. Later, the shrub graph mistakenly changed to be 刀, knife, and the radical 井, 艸（草）was added to indicate phonetic meaning.

177

# 竟 jìng

〔附〕境 jìng

In oracle bone inscriptions, the character was not formed by 音 and 人, but above 人 was 辛 (a punishment knife), meaning to make a mark on the neck of a slave by the knife, and the finish of the job was called 竟. The original meaning was "to finish," "to end." It was interchangeable with 境.

甲骨文

金文

小篆

隶书

楷书

草书

行书

简化字

（同楷书）

178

# 纠 (糾 糺) jiū

The original form was written as 丩. In oracle bone inscriptions and bronze inscriptions, the graph was both like two ropes wound with each other. A variant form of the character was 糺. Today's standard character has become 纠.

# 久 jiǔ

久 was the primitive form of 灸. Graphically, it was a man lying on his side and a 艾炷, moxa cone, placed on his back as a medical treatment. Later, it is mostly loaned to indicate 时间长久, long time.

甲骨文 （缺）

金文 久

小篆 久

隶书 久

楷书 久

草书 久

行书 久

简化字 （同楷书）

# 灸 jiǔ

According to *Suo Wen*, it was made up of 火 and 久, meaning "to burn." In fact, 久 was the primitive form of 灸, which is a way of medical treatment in Chinese medicine (see character 久). 灸 also means 烧灼, burn or scorch. Do not mistake it for 炙, zhì, to roast.

（缺）

古玺文

小篆

隶书

楷书

草书

行书

简化字

（同楷书）

181

# 臼 jiù

As a utensil for pounding rice, graphically, it looked like a section drawing of 臼 of which the middle short slanting lines represented 米, rice. In the *Book of Change*, it was said that "the one for cutting wood was 杵; the one for digging earth was 臼."

# 咎 jiù

Graphically in oracle bone inscriptions, it was a vivid delineation that a large foot, which might symbolize a heavenly god or a ruler determining one's life and death, was stepping onto a little man. In a word, it meant "misfortune befalls." It extends to mean "ominous calamity," "crime," "look into," etc.

甲骨文

金文

小篆

隶书

楷书

草书

行书

简化字

（同楷书）

183

掬 jū

The original form was 匊, composing of 米 and 勹 which was the form wrongly deriving from that of an arm. Its graph would be a hand holding a handful of rice. The initial meaning is "to fully hold," "to completely hold in two hands."

匊

匊

掬

掬

掬

掬

（同楷书）

# 局 jú

Its initial meaning is "chessboard," and 局子 is chessman. Its grapheme is quite like a chessman, among which 口 is its pedestal. Later, it is loaned to mean 局促, uneasy, 局部, part, 局面, situation, and 官署名, the name for a government office, etc.

（缺）

甲骨文

局

秦简文

局

小篆

局

隶书

局

楷书

局

草书

局

行书

（同楷书）

简化字

185

# 巨 jù

〔附〕矩 jǔ

巨 was the initial form of 矩（also as 榘）. The meaning was "the carpenter's square ruler." In bronze inscriptions it was in the form that a man was measuring with an I-shaped square ruler.

甲骨文

金文

小篆

隶书

楷书

草书

行书

简化字

（缺）

（同楷书）

186

# 惧（懼）jù

〔附〕瞿 jù, Qú

It was initially written as 䀠 (see character 瞿). Later, 心 was added to indicate "the fear from the heart." It extended to mean "to fear or frightened." It was interchangeable with 瞿. Its simplified version has 具 as the sound radical.

（缺）

| 甲骨文 |
| --- |
| 说文『古文』 |
| 小篆 |
| 隶书 |
| 楷书 |
| 草书 |
| 行书 |
| 简化字 |

# 绝（絕）jué

It primitively meant "the broken silk." In oracle bone inscriptions, it was a bundle of silk that had been cut off by three sharp tools. Otherwise, in bronze inscriptions, it had a 刀-shape added to it. In small seal characters, the right radical was 刀, or 卩 (人-shaped form). In regular script, its right part was wrongly turned into 色, which is hard to trace its origin.

# 军（軍）jūn

    "Army" is the original meaning of the character, which is made up of 車 (army carts, referring to arms), and 匀 (as a phonetic symbol. However, in small seal characters it wrongly altered to be 勹; in official script it changed again to be 冖). It also signified a unit of army.

| | |
|---|---|
| 甲骨文 | （缺） |
| 金文 | 軍 |
| 小篆 | 軍 |
| 隶书 | 軍 |
| 楷书 | 軍 |
| 草书 | 軍 |
| 行书 | 軍 |
| 简化字 | 军 |

# 钧（鈞）jūn

〔附〕匀 yún

钧 was a heavy unit in ancient times. It was originally written as 匀; it was added 金（see character 金）as a form to invent 鈞（钧）. Hence, it has "pottery wheels," "music tune," and other meanings. It can still be used as an honorific term such as 钧座, Your Honor.

| 甲骨文 | （缺） |
| --- | --- |
| 金文 | 匀 |
| 小篆 | 鈞 |
| 隶书 | 鈞 |
| 楷书 | 鈞 |
| 草书 | 钧 |
| 行书 | 钧 |
| 简化字 | 钧 |

190

# 均 jūn

〔附〕韵（韻）yùn

With the composition of 土 and 匀 (signifying a meaning of "on average") as the sound symbol, its original meaning was "average-distributed," "fair." It extends to indicate "universal," "adjust," "equal to," etc. It was interchangeable with 韵（韻）and in ancient times 均 replaced 韵.

# 开（開）kāi

From its earlier form of the character such a vivid scene could be seen that in the middle of two doors a hand was pulling a latch. But after small seal characters, it became awkward to understand its form. The primitive meaning was "to open the door."

（缺）

閞

開

開

開

开

闬

开

# 刊 kān

（缺）

（同楷书）

Originally written as 枻 （in *Suo Wen*, the above part was the form of two 天, which is in doubt）and composed of 木 and 幵 （meaning "the upper part flat"）, the original meaning was 削, to chop or cut. It extended to indicate "to carve," "to make corrections." Later, it altered to be a phonogram with the pronunciation of 干.

193

看 kàn, kān

甲骨文 （缺）

金文 （缺）

It was "to watch" originally. Under the sun, in order to see clearly, people often shade their heads with hands. 看 is just one to express such a meaning with 目, eyes, and 手. It extends to mean "to call on somebody," "to visit," "to regard as," etc. When meaning 守护, to guard, it is pronounced kān.

小篆 看

隶书 看

楷书 看

草书 看

行书 看

简化字 （同楷书）

194

# 科 kē

〔附〕棵 kē

The primitive meaning was "category" or "class". This is an associate compound character: i. e. to measure 禾, plants, with 斗, a unit of dry measure for grains, in order to differentiate the categories of grain. With a great variety of meanings of 科, one of which is a measure word as 棵 today.

195

# 可 kě

It is composed of 丂 (the original form of 柯, meaning ax handle and signifying sound) and 口 (indicating the oral permission, the oral affirmation). It extends to mean "to be able to," "be worthy of," "be suitable to," etc.

甲骨文

金文

小篆

隶书

楷书

草书

行书

简化字

（同楷书）

196

# 肯 kěn

It was written as 冎 originally. Its meaning was "flesh attached to the bones." 冖 was the simplified version of 骨; 月 i.e. 肉, indicated the joint of bones and flesh. Later, it was often loaned as 可.

197

# 孔 kǒng

Its original meaning was "nipple."
It was in the form of a baby sucking
breast milk in bronze inscriptions. It further indicated the nipples of other animals. Its extended meanings are "understanding or sensible," and "big,"
"fine," "very," etc.

甲骨文

金文

小篆

隶书

楷书

草书

行书

简化字

（同楷书）

198

# 恐 kǒng

The character was originally composed of 心 and 工 (as a phonetic symbol). Later, its phonetic radical 工 changed into 巩. The initial meaning was 惧, i.e. in dread of, or to fear. It extends to mean 恐怕, be afraid of. It still has the meaning of 恐吓, to frighten.

（缺）

甲骨文

金文

小篆

隶书

楷书

草书

行书

简化字

（同楷书）

199

# 寇 kòu

In a house, a trespasser was taking a wood stab and hitting the head of the owner. The initial meaning was "to exert violence on," "to rob and seize." Another meaning is "robber."

甲骨文

金文

小篆

隶书

楷书

草书

行书

简化字

（同楷书）

200

# 哭 kū

金文

小篆

隶书

楷书

草书

行书

简化字

（同楷书）

Why did 哭 in regular script have a radical of 犬? It's hard to give an explanation. However, in oracle bone inscriptions, the middle part of the character was a man with his hair spreading disorderly; the two sides were 吅 (the same meaning and sounding as 喧）. With the two it meant a person who was wailing.

# 库（庫）kù

The character meant "a place where army carriages were stored," and it was constituted of placing 车 under 广. The radical 广, sounded as yǎn, means a house built by the mountain cliff as to store warring carriages and weapons for its cover and shelter. Later, it extensively refers to "a grain depot," "a currency storehouse," etc.

（缺）

甲骨文

金文　庫

小篆　庫

隶书　庫

楷书　庫

草书　庫

行书　庫

简化字　库

# 块（塊）kuài

The original form was 凷, and its original meaning, "earth clods." The graph was in the shape of a basket full of clods. Since the time of small seal characters, the character 塊 began to emerge and it gradually came into use and replaced 凷.

甲骨文

金文

小篆

隶书

楷书

草书

行书

简化字

凷

凷

凷

塊

塊

塊

块

# 狂 kuáng

The original meaning was "mad dog." It was initially composed of 犬 ( 犭 ) and 垈 ( i. e. 往, signifying sound ). It extended to indicate "mad or insane," or even "wildly arrogant," "indulge in," "monstrous," etc.

甲骨文

金文

小篆

隶书

楷书

草书

行书

简化字

犲

犲

犲

狂

狟

狂

（同楷书）

204

# 昆 kūn

昆 originally meant 同, the same. It extends to mean "elder brother of the same parents." 兄弟 once was written as and called 昆仲. It also takes on the meanings of 众, numerous, and 昆虫, all the insects.

（缺）

（同楷书）

# 困 kùn

While entering a yard, the first thing made of wood is the doorsill — 梱, which originated from 困 as its original form. For the limit of a doorsill it can extend to mean "hardship," "embarrassment," "besiege," etc.

说文『古文』

小篆

隶书

楷书

草书

行书

简化字

（同楷书）

# 离 (離) lí

〔附〕 罹 lí

The grapheme in oracle bone inscriptions was a net with a long shaft having caught a bird. The original meaning was "to catch birds." It extends to indicate "to suffer disaster," "meet with misfortune," and was interchangeable with 罹. In the later days, it was loaned to be the name for a bird, i.e. 黄鹂, oriole, another name, 黄莺.

甲骨文

金文

小篆

隶书

楷书

草书

行书

简化字

207

# 厘 (釐) lí

The form in oracle bone inscriptions was a hand holding a wand striking wheat grains to have them threshed. It indicated "harvesting," i.e. "blissful." Later, the radical 里 was added to indicate its sound. In ancient books it was mostly loaned to mean 治理, managing or running, 改变, change, 分开, divide, and also used as a length unit (equals to 0.013 inch or so). The simplified 厘 was already seen in the Eastern Jin Dynasty (317 – 420 A.D.).

208

# 礼（禮）lǐ

It was primitively written as 豊. Its graph in oracle bone inscriptions looked like two strings of precious jades in a ceremonial container for worshipping gods. Later, because of its similar form to 豊（丰）, the two characters were often confused in use, hence, the radical 示（indicating a sacrificial table）was added to form 禮. It originally meant 敬神, worshipping gods, such as 礼神.

209

# 里₁ lǐ

Made up of 田 and 土, it primitively meant "the place where human beings live." It extends to mean "homeland." It can also be used as a length unit, i.e. one *li* equals to a half kilometer. The simplified version also substitutes for 裏.

里₂(裏裡) ⟨II⟩

It is a phonogram. The exterior is 衣 (a semantic symbol) and the interior is 里 (a phonetic symbol). The original meaning was "the inside layer of clothing." It extends to indicate "inside," "within," against "outside," "exterior." Today, the current 裏 has been simplified and combined to 里.

211

# 怜（憐）lián

Originally composed of 心（meaning）and 舛（sounding, see character 磷）, it meant "to sympathize with," "to take pity on." It again had a meaning of 爱, love, which is not contained in modern Chinese language.

（缺）

# 良 liáng

〔附〕郎 láng 廊 láng

Its initial meaning was 廊, corridor. Afterwards, it was written as 郎, 廊. The graph in oracle bone inscriptions was a square pavilion in the middle and the upper and the lower part each like a corridor. 良 was often used to mean "virtue," "beauty and fine," "wisdom," and others in ancient writings.

| 甲骨文 |
| 金文 |
| 小篆 |
| 隶书 |
| 楷书 |
| 草书 |
| 行书 |
| 简化字 |

（同楷书）

213

# 梁（樑）liáng

〔附〕梁 liáng

From the bronze inscriptions of the early Western Zhou Dynasty, the character didn't take 木 but an ideograph of a bridge by 水（river）. The original meaning was "a river bridge." Since small seal characters, the radical 木 was added. However, in regular script, some variant form even had two 木 as 樑. Sometimes it was interchangeable with 梁.

214

# 量 liáng, liàng

At first, the character was constituted of 日 and 重 (see character 重), meaning to measure the weight of objects under the sun. The original meaning is "to measure weight or length with the measuring tools." It extends to mean "to evaluate," "to consult with," ( pronounced liáng). But in 度量衡, metrology, 容器, container, 器量, magnanimity, it is pronounced as liàng.

| | |
|---|---|
| 甲骨文 | （缺） |
| 金文 | |
| 小篆 | |
| 隶书 | |
| 楷书 | |
| 草书 | |
| 行书 | |
| 简化字 | （同楷书） |

215

# 两（兩）liǎng

〔附〕辆（輛）liàng

The earlier form looked like a yoke and a pair of saddles of a two-horse carriage. The initial meaning was "two," or "double." It was also a unit to count vehicles and written as 辆 later.

甲骨文

金文

小篆

隶书

楷书

草书

行书

简化字

# 料 liào

金文

小篆

隶书

楷书

草书

行书

简化字

（同楷书）

料 meant 量, to measure. How much weight is called 量 and how many is called 料. It extended to mean "sort and count." Also it extends to mean "predicate," "guess," "select," "manage," etc. Once more, it is used to refer to "wood material," "raw material," "historical data," etc.

217

# 临（臨）lín

With his eyes widely open, a man was overlooking several objects on the ground. The original meaning was "to look down from a high place." Its extends to indicate 降临, befall. It also extends to mean "to rule," "to approach," "to face."

218

# 磷 lín

It was written as 粦 (㷠). Its original meaning was 磷火, phosphorescent light, namely 鬼火, ghost fire. Due to its inconstancy, phosphorescent light seemed to be walking at night. Hence, the graph of the lower part in bronze inscriptions was a pair of feet.

金文

粦

小篆

粦

隶书

磷

楷书

磷

草书

磷

行书

磷

简化字

（同楷书）

219

# 霖 lín

The initial meaning was "raining for long time," of which 雨 indicated meaning and 林, referring to the forest, indicated its pronunciation.

220

# 陵 líng

Graphically in oracle bone inscriptions, it was a man ascending the hill on the stone steps (see character 阜). Its original meaning was "a large earth hill," and still has the meanings of "to ascend," "to rise." It extends to mean "the tombs of emperors and kings," "exceed," "intrude and insult," etc.

料

陵 陵

陵 陵

陵 陵

陵

（同楷书）

221

# 零 líng

〔附〕霝 líng

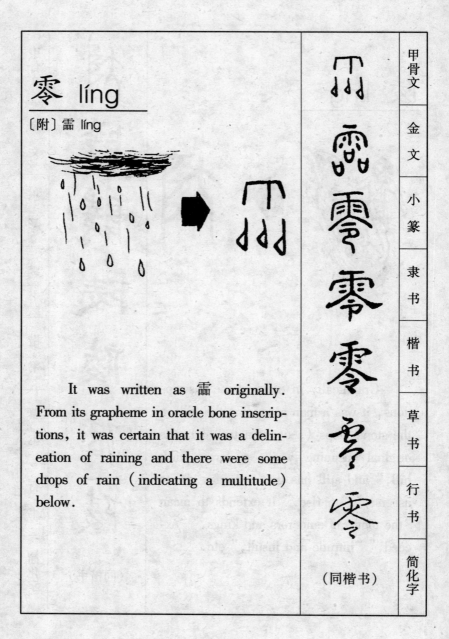

It was written as 霝 originally. From its grapheme in oracle bone inscriptions, it was certain that it was a delineation of raining and there were some drops of rain（indicating a multitude）below.

甲骨文

金文

小篆

隶书

楷书

草书

行书

简化字

（同楷书）

222

# 灵 (靈) líng

The original meaning was "gods." Primitively, the upper part was 霝 (see character 零), signifying the meaning of drizzling and also sounding; the lower part in bronze inscriptions was 示 (a sacrificial table), 王 (玉) or 心. Only in small seal characters, there appeared a variant form with the character of 巫, especially meaning "a dancing and pleading-god necromancer."

| | |
|---|---|
| 甲骨文 | （缺） |
| 金文 | 霝示 |
| 小篆 | 靈 |
| 隶书 | 靈 |
| 楷书 | 靈 |
| 草书 | 靈 |
| 行书 | 靈 |
| 简化字 | 灵 |

223

# 卢（盧）lú

〔附〕炉（爐鑪）lú 庐（廬）lú

It was the original form of 炉, stove. The lower part of the character in oracle bone inscriptions was like a stove; the upper part was 虍 (tiger's head, pronounced hū, signifying sound). In bronze inscriptions, 皿 was added to indicate the loan meaning of "meal utensils." Due to the dark color smoked by both fire and smokes, 卢 has a meaning of "black or dark." It was interchangeable with 庐.

甲骨文
金文
小篆
隶书
楷书
草书
行书
简化字

# 卤（鹵）lǔ

The original meaning is "the raw salt without being processed." It extends to indicate 盐碱地, saline area.

225

履 lǚ

It initially meant "walking on foot," and also had the meaning of "shoes." From the earliest grapheme, it was composed of 頁 (head, indicating man), 舟 (boat, signifying going ahead) and 正 (the variant of 止, i.e. 趾, indicating foot), expressing to advance on foot. Later, its form changed a great deal.

（缺）

頿

履

屨

履

覆

履

（同楷书）

# 率 lǜ, shuài

率（lǜ）initially meant "thick rope," and was the original form of 繂. It looked like a piece of rope in both oracle bone inscriptions and bronze inscriptions; the nearby dots were flax scraps left while pulling. The bird-catching net made by such ropes was called 率（shuài）.

甲骨文

金文

小篆

隶书

楷书

草书

行书

简化字

（同楷书）

卵 luǎn

The ova or spawns of some insects, frogs and fish are always the eggs that many little ones are inside being enclosed by thin membranes. The character 卵 is just endowed with such a meaning by having two eggs together.

（缺）

甲骨文

战国文字

小篆

隶书

楷书

草书

行书

简化字

（同楷书）

# 乱（亂）luàn

It was initially written as 𤔔. Graphically in bronze inscriptions it was a bundle of disordered silk and an upper hand and a lower hand were just combing it. Silk is difficult to be put in order. Hence, the original meaning is 紊乱, fouling-up. Its extended meaning is 不安定, instability.

# 麻（蔴）má

People are usually drying hemp under the mountain cliff（厂, appeared in bronze inscriptions）or the eave（广, in small seal characters, etc.）. 麻 in ancient times only referred to cannabis. Later, 艹 was added to invent 蔴, and its simplified version has combined to 麻.

230

# 埋 mái

〔附〕霾 mái

埋 was the original form of 霾. It originally meant "dust blown by wind, just like raining dust," so it had 雨 as a form. 貍 was 狐狸, fox, and for its sound similarity in ancient times, it was loaned to indicate sound. It extended to mean "to cover up," "to bury." 埋 began to appear at much later time.

霿

霾

埋

埋

埋

埋

（同楷书）

231

# 曼 màn

The primitive meaning was 展开, to spread. It extended to indicate "extending," "long-term." In oracle bone inscriptions, it looked like two hands covering the head to see further. In bronze inscriptions, 曰 (帽, later mistakenly changing to 日) was added as a phonetic symbol.

（同楷书）

232

# 莽 mǎng

Its graph was like a dog crouching in the grass. The primitive meaning was "thickly growing grass." It also referred to common grass. It extended to mean "large," "expansive." Again, it extended to mean "rough and careless," "reckless."

（缺）

甲骨文

金文

小篆

隶书

楷书

草书

行书

简化字

（同楷书）

# 矛 máo

矛 is an ancient weapon which can stab forward. It has a long shaft, with an ear on one side or each side so that the ropes can be through to tightly tie the warring carriage vertically.

（缺）

甲骨文

金文

小篆

隶书

楷书

草书

行书

简化字

（同楷书）

234

# 毛 máo

In bronze inscriptions, 毛 was like a feather of a bird. In *Suo Wen*, it meant the brow hair or the hair of animals. It was an ideograph. The hair of man or animals is called 毛 and birds' hair is called 羽, feather; both are called 毛 in general.

（同楷书）

235

# 卯 mǎo

It was the original form of 窌, i.e. cellar, a cavity or a pit for storing food. Later, it was used to indicate the fourth of the Earthly Branches and to count years, months, or hours.

（同楷书）

236

# 冒 mào

〔附〕帽 mào

It was the initial form of 帽, hat or cap. It was made up of 冃 (the graph of a cap, not 曰) and 目 (eyes, representing the face). It extends to mean "to cover," "to carry on the head," "backbone malefactors," "to pretend to be," etc.

（缺）

（同楷书）

237

# 枚 méi

The original meaning was 树干, trunk. From the early form of bronze inscriptions, it was seen obviously that a hand was holding a big ax cutting a tree. 条 indicates branches and 枚 indicates trunks. It is mostly used as a measure word, equaling to 个, a piece of.

（同楷书）

238

# 妹 mèi

With the composition of 女 and 未 ( as a phonetic symbol ), the original meaning was "younger sisters of the same parents." It extended to indicate "young girls."

（同楷书）

239

# 媚 mèi

A girl with beautiful brows and eyes is really pretty and lovely. 眉 also indicates sound. Hence, 媚 has the meaning of "charming," and "lovely," too.

甲骨文

金文

小篆

隶书

楷书

草书

行书

简化字

（同楷书）

240

# 盟 méng

It primitively meant 结盟, to form an alliance. In oracle bone inscriptions, it was made up of 囧 (meaning a bright window, pronounced jiǒng and also míng) and 皿. When the ancient dukes allied, they firstly killed livestock for blood and filled the vessels with wine, and then took an oath to gods. Hence, the character was constructed by the form of 皿. Some other versions have the form of 血 and it is also understandable.

| | |
|---|---|
| 甲骨文 | |
| 金文 | |
| 小篆 | |
| 隶书 | |
| 楷书 | |
| 草书 | |
| 行书 | |
| 简化字 | （同楷书） |

# 孟 mèng

It was constituted of 子 (a semantic symbol) and 皿 (indicating meaning in most other characters but here as a sound symbol). The original meaning was "the eldest one of brothers and sisters." It extended to indicate the first month of each season. Also as a family name, e.g. 孟子（孟轲）, Mencius.

| 甲骨文 | （缺） |
|---|---|
| 金文 | 𤔔 |
| 小篆 | 𤔔 孟 |
| 隶书 | 孟 |
| 楷书 | 孟 |
| 草书 | 孟 |
| 行书 | 孟 |
| 简化字 | （同楷书） |

242

# 梦（夢）mèng

A man was dreaming lying in bed （a number of forms of the characters in oracle bone inscriptions were written vertically）, "with his eyes open" he seemed to be seeing the things in his dream. It is also written as 寢.

# 冕 miǎn

〔附〕免 miǎn

It was originally written as 免, whose grapheme was like a man wearing a very large hat. The primitive meaning was "the hat worn by ancient emperors and kings, dukes, feudal ministers and officials." Later, it only referred to "emperor's crown or coronal," such as coronation ceremeny. Otherwise, 免 has become a character of quite different significance.

（同楷书）

244

# 面（麵麪）miàn

面 in oracle bone inscriptions was just in the form of a portrait painted by a western modern abstractionist: only one eye was given prominence to and a rhombic frame was drawn outside. In simplified characters, 麵（麪）is combined to 面.

（同楷书）

# 苗 miáo

The character is made up of 艹 (草) and 田, indicating seedlings of plants are growing out of the field. The original meaning referred to "the seed plants at their early periods." It extends to indicate "some newly born animals," e.g. 鱼苗, fry.

| | |
|---|---|
| 甲骨文 | （缺） |
| 金文 | |
| 小篆 | |
| 隶书 | |
| 楷书 | |
| 草书 | |
| 行书 | |
| 简化字 | （同楷书） |

246

# 蔑 (衊) miè

The primitive meaning was "to die out." It was originally composed of 眉 (a phonetic symbol) and 伐 (a semantic symbol). It extended to indicate "cast away," "look down on," "insult," etc. In simplified characters, 衊 is also combined to 蔑.

甲骨文

金文

小篆

隶书

楷书

草书

行书

简化字

(同楷书)

247

# 民 mín

〔附〕岷 máng

Modern people may not believe that 民 originally meant "slaves," and even those who had been captives and then were forced to be slaves after their left eyes stabbed blind with sharp tools by slaveholders. The graphic form in bronze inscriptions has already proved this. Later, it referred to 百姓, civilians or common people. It was also written as 岷.

（同楷书）

甲骨文　金文　小篆　隶书　楷书　草书　行书　简化字

248

# 末 mò

The original meaning is "treetop." Its meaning is just against that of 本, end (see character 本). Its self-explanatory symbol in bronze inscriptions was "the end of a tree," symbolizing the place of a treetop. Later, it extends to mean 尽头, end, 末尾, last, 终了, ending, 最后, in the end, etc.

（缺）

（同楷书）

牟 móu, mù

牟 indicated cattle lowing original-ly. The character has 牛 as a radical as if the voice was coming out of its mouth. The upper spiral sign on the ox's head indicates long lowing from low voice to high voice. In the modern Chinese, it is mostly loaned to use as 牟利, obtain un-reasonable profits, and others.

（缺）

（同楷书）

250

# 某 mǒu

〔附〕梅 méi

某, the original form of 梅, was composed of 木 and 甘. This is an associate compound character. It was often loaned to use as an indicative pronoun, such as 某人, somebody, 某地, somewhere; it can also indicate 自己, oneself.

| | |
|---|---|
| 甲骨文 | （缺） |
| 金文 | 𣉺 |
| 小篆 | 某 |
| 隶书 | 某 |
| 楷书 | 某 |
| 草书 | 某 |
| 行书 | 某 |
| 简化字 | （同楷书） |

251

# 牡 mǔ

It is the common name for all the male animals (the female is called 牝). In oracle bone inscriptions, 丄（土）was a symbol to represent male animals and primitively used to invent new characters with 牛，羊，马，豕, etc. Finally, all such characters were combined to 牡.

（同楷书）

252

# 耐 nài

It was a light punishment in ancient times, i.e. the whiskers of a mistake-taking official were shaved off as to put him to shame. The left part of the character is 而, whiskers (see character 而); the right one is 寸（又）, a hand. Later, it indicates the meaning of "being able to endure," and others.

253

# 能 néng

〔附〕熊 xióng

甲骨文 金文 小篆 隶书 楷书 草书 行书 简化字

It was the original form of 熊, bear. The grapheme in bronze inscriptions resembled the shape of a bear. Later, 能 was loaned to mainly mean 才能, talent, 贤能, wisdom, 能够, be able to, etc., hence, another character 熊 was invented to convey the original meaning.

（同楷书）

254

# 尼 ní

〔附〕昵（暱）nì

➡

It was the primitive form of 昵（暱）. Graphically it took the shape of two persons leaning on one another. It initially meant 亲昵, very intimate，亲近, intimate. It extended to indicate 安, safety. Later, it referred to the females who practice Buddhism.

（缺）

甲骨文

古玺文

小篆

隶书

楷书

草书

行书

简化字

（同楷书）

255

# 辇（輦）niǎn

It is a cart pulled or pushed by people. The early grapheme in bronze inscriptions was visually delineated that two persons were pulling a cart. After the Qin and Han dynasties, it exclusively referred to the vehicles for emperors, kings and imperial concubines. Also, it extended to indicate "to carry," and others.

甲骨文

金文

小篆

隶书

楷书

草书

行书

简化字

# 奴 nú

A big hand held a woman and forced her to be a slave. 奴 originally meant "slaves" (including both males and females). Later, it mostly indicated 仆人, servants.

甲骨文

金文

小篆

隶书

楷书

草书

行书

简化字

（同楷书）

257

# 怒 nù

There are a great number of phonograms in chinese, for example, the character with "奴" in the upper part and "心" in the lower part. It does not mean "the heart of a slave." This is 怒 meaning "being angry." It extends to be "much vigorous," "exerting oneself."

（缺）

（同楷书）

甲骨文

战国文字

小篆

隶书

楷书

草书

行书

简化字

# 虐 nüè

Its primitive meaning was "cruel-ly kill." The upper part of it is a tiger's head (虍); the lower both a tiger's claw and a little man. It extends to mean 残暴, inhumanity, and also 过分, ex-cess, etc.

甲骨文

秦石文

小篆

隶书

楷书

草书

行书

简化字

（缺）

（同楷书）

259

# 偶 ǒu

It is a phonogram, constituting of
人（indicating meaning）and 禺（a
sound symbol, meaning a long-tailed
monkey）. The primitive meaning was
"man's statue made of wood or earth."
Its extended meanings are 同辈, of the
same generation, 配对, to match, 配
偶, spouse, 双数, even numbers, etc.

（缺）

禺

偶

偶

偶

偶

偶

（同楷书）

甲骨文

金文

小篆

隶书

楷书

草书

行书

简化字

260

# 佩 pèi

Its original meaning is "adornments attached to the clothing belts." 凡 represents sound and 巾 indicates meaning for it is a kind of clothes or something. It extends to indicate "to wear or put on," "to take or carry." Furthermore, it extends to mean 钦仰, respect and admire, etc.

（同楷书）

# 皮 pí

〔附〕彼 bǐ

Its original meaning is "to peel off the skin." It also refers to "the exterior skins of plants or animals." The graph in bronze inscriptions was a hand peeling off the skin of a dead animal with its mouth widely open and its skin stood out. It was interchangeable with 彼 in ancient times.

# 匹 pǐ

（缺）

（同楷书）

It was the unit of length for measuring cloth and it was the same as four 丈 (one 丈 is about 3.3 meters). Its graph was like sunning cloth on the foot of the cliff. While measuring the cloth, the two ends of the cloth had to be rolled up sometimes and one 匹 contained two 卷, so it has got the meanings of 匹偶, spouse, 对手, a rival, etc. It is also the unit to count horses.

263

# 辟₂（闢）pì

In bronze inscriptions, it was a pair of hands opening the door. This is an associate compound character. Since the beginning of small seal characters, there began to appear a phonogram with the forms of 门 and 辟 (as a sound symbol). The original meaning was "to open," "unseal." It extends to indicate 开拓, set up, 排除, eliminate, etc. 闢 has been simplified and combined to 辟.

（缺）

| | |
|---|---|
| 甲骨文 | （缺） |
| 金文 | |
| 小篆 | |
| 隶书 | |
| 楷书 | |
| 草书 | |
| 行书 | |
| 简化字 | 辟 |

264

# 片 piàn

Its original meaning is "to cut wood into something thin and flat." In oracle bone inscriptions, its graph was two (indicating many) slight pieces cut from a half of wood, 木 (tree). In modern Chinese language, it still follows to convey the same sense, such as 木片, pieces of wood, 竹片, bamboo pieces, 名片, name cards. It is also used as a measure word.

甲骨文

金文

小篆

隶书

楷书

草书

行书

简化字

（同楷书）

265

# 牝 pìn

It is a common name of all the female animals（the male is 牡）. In oracle bone inscriptions，匕 was a symbol for female animals and originally used to make other characters with 牛，羊，马，豕，etc.，and later all such characters were combined to 牝.

（缺）

（同楷书）

266

# 漆 qī

➡

The character was originally written as 桼, and its form was like a tree with tree juices dropping. Besides, in the simplified versions, it is often loaned to replace 七, seven. 漆 firstly was the name for a branch of the Wei River in the area of Shanxi Province. Later, this character has replaced 桼.

（缺）

（同楷书）

| 甲骨文 | 战国文字 | 小篆 | 隶书 | 楷书 | 草书 | 行书 | 简化字 |

妻 qī

Woman's long hair could only be touched by her husband, so such a case was in oracle bone inscriptions to indicate the notion of 妻, wife. Otherwise, it could be also explained by the custom that the bridegroom pretended to kidnap his bride in primitive times.

甲骨文

金文

小篆

隶书

楷书

草书

行书

简化字

（同楷书）

# 旗 qí

（同楷书）

In oracle bone inscriptions, this character was like a flag. 旗 has some other variants such as 㫃 (pronounced yǎn in the old times), 旂 (pronounced qí). In oracle bone inscriptions, the character 㫃 was obviously a flag waving on the flagpole; since the time of bronze inscriptions, 斤 (ax, indicating weapon) or 其 (indicating sound) as a form to constitute 旂 and 旗 to share the same meaning.

# 企 qǐ

A man is standing there with his big feet extruded. The original meaning was "to stand on tiptoe." It has a meaning of "standing," too. In modern Chinese language, some dialects still use 企 to express "standing." It extends to mean "to look forward to," "to desire for," etc.

甲骨文

说文『古文』

小篆

隶书

楷书

草书

行书

简化字

（同楷书）

# 器 qì

In bronze inscriptions, the shape of the character was a dog in the middle, and four 口 nearby. The character with four 口 mostly takes on the meaning of 喧哗, roaring, hence, it can be deduced that it was the primitive form of 狋 (also 狺, dog's barking). However, with the primitive meaning not existent, generally it is loaned to mean 器具, equipment or tools, 器官, organs, or others.

# 契 qì

It was the original form of 栔, like carving marks on the bamboo pieces with a knife. The original meaning was "to carve with a knife." Later, 大 or 木 was added. Its extended meanings are 证明文书, certificates and writs, 兵符, army tokens, 投合, agree or cater to, and others.

（同楷书）

272

# 牵（牽）qiān

〔附〕纤（縴）qiàn

Composed of 玄 (can be regarded as a rope, indicting meaning), 冂 (as a bullpen), and 牛, it signifies "to pull an ox out of the bullpen by rope." It also means "the tugs for pulling boats." Later, it is written as 縴（纤）.

金文

小篆

隶书

楷书

草书

行书

简化字

# 遣 qiǎn

Graphically in oracle bone inscriptions, it was two hands holding a handful of earth (𠂤, see character 堆) and filling it in a container (some grapheme without hands). It had been the name for sacrificial offering. Later, it had a radical of 辵 (indicating action) to symbolize "to release," "to dispatch," etc.

（同楷书）

274

# 浅（淺）qiǎn

This is a phonogram. It initially meant "not deep," and was composed of 水 and 戔. The character 戔（戋）seemed to be two 戈（an ancient weapon）up and down, whose original meaning was "to cruelly kill," but only functioned as a phonetic symbol here.

（缺）

甲骨文

金文

小篆

隶书

楷书

草书

行书

简化字

275

# 墙 （墙牆）qiáng

The character was made up of 嗇 (the original form of 穡, meaning to harvest grains. See character 嗇), and 爿 (the original form of 床, as a sound symbol. See character 床), signifying to build walls to store grains.

# 乔（喬）qiáo

In *Suo Wen*, the character meant "high and bent." However, there were several variants in bronze inscriptions, and one of them similar to the above explanation was the case that a curve hook graph was on the top of the character 高. After small seal characters, it wrongly evolved itself into one of 夭 or 高, with the latter's form somewhat simplified.

# 琴 qín

（缺）

（同楷书）

琴, a kind of stringed music instrument in ancient times, had seven strings. It was initially a pictograph: the arc shape indicated the body of the instrument, the horizontal line indicated the strings and the middle vertical line indicated the column; later 金 or 今 was added to indicate sound. (See character 瑟.)

278

# 青 qīng

金文

小篆

隶书

楷书

草书

行书

简化字

青
青
青
青
青
青

（同楷书）

The character was constituted of 丹 （硃砂, cinnabar, representing color） and 生（representing sound）. The original meaning was "the color when things beganto grow," i.e. the green color when grass and wood began budding in spring. It also referred to the blue color, such as 青天, and the black color, such as 青丝（black hair）. It extends to mean "young," and so on.

279

# 顷（頃）qǐng

〔附〕倾（傾）qīng

顷 was the original form of 倾, meaning "the head not being straight or upright." It was made of 匕 (the converse form of 人) and 页 (man's head). It extended to indicate 倾斜, slant.

280

# 庆（慶）qìng

When the ancient people congratulated someone on a happy event or occasion, they often sent him a piece of deerskin as a gift to express their kindly feelings. Hence, it was originally constituted of 鹿 and 心, and its initial meaning was "to congratulate." It extends to indicate 善, goodness, 福, happiness, and so on.

甲骨文
金文
小篆
隶书
楷书
草书
行书
简化字

281

# 磬 qìng

The character graphically in oracle bone inscriptions was a hand with a small hammer striking a musical instrument hung by a piece of rope, 殸. Since small seal characters, it has been added 石 as a form to it, for the instrument was made of materials such as jades or stones.

（同楷书）

282

# 酋 qiú

The initial meaning was 掌酒官, a person in charge of distributing liquors or wines. It was composed of 八, to divide, and 酉, wine or liquor. In ancient times, the person, who was in charge of the job concerning wines or liquors and distributing them to drinkers, was named 大酋. Later, it extended to mean "the chief of a tribe." Today, 酋长, is still in use.

瞿 Qú, jù

It was originally written as 睍 . The initial meaning was "being frightened when seeing something." Later, the radical 隹（鸟）was added to invent 瞿 .

（缺）

甲骨文

金文

小篆

隶书

楷书

草书

行书

简化字

（同楷书）

284

# 然 rán

〔附〕燃 rán

然 was the primitive form of 燃. The meaning was "to burn." It was made up of 火，犬，月（肉），meaning "to roast the dog's meat on the fire." But in ancient books it was often loaned to mean 许诺，promise，如此，so，such，as it is，是，yes，and also as a function word.

（缺）

（同楷书）

285

# 仁 rén

It is constituted of 人 and 二, a-mong which 二 is not only regarded as a symbol for repetition but also indicates 人 different from 从（從）. The original meaning of 仁 was "to intimate people." Subsequently, it evolved into "a widely meaningful moral category," such as 仁爱, "kindheartedness," 仁政, "benev-olent politics," etc. advocated by the Confucianists.

甲骨文

金文

小篆

隶书

楷书

草书

行书

简化字

（同楷书）

# 刃 rèn

The original meaning is 刀口, i.e. the sharpest part of a knife or a sword. This is a typical self-explanatory character, and the dot by the blade is a self-explanatory symbol itself. It extends to indicate "knife," "sword," etc. It also extends to mean "to kill or murder."

甲骨文

金文

小篆

隶书

楷书

草书

行书

简化字

（同楷书）

287

# 荣（榮）róng

〔附〕荧（熒）yíng 萤（螢）yíng

The graph in bronze inscriptions was obviously two crossed torches, which was the primitive form of 荣（榮）and 荧（熒）. They were originally the same one character, meaning "bright." 荧 was also identical to 萤（螢）.

288

# 容 róng

Its original meaning was "to contain and then place," or "hide." The earlier form appeared to put the objects（口）onto a place like a cave or something. It also contains the meanings of "capacity," "appearance," and so on.

（同楷书）

# 肉 ròu

肉 was like a slice of neatly cut meat in oracle bone inscriptions. However, in bronze inscriptions and small seal characters, the graph took the likeness of 月, moon, on which the slanting lines seemed to be marks of the ribs. After official script it became not very pictographic. As a radical, 肉 and 月 have been confused in usage with each other, and their difference can only be deduced from their own meanings and origins.

甲骨文

金文

小篆

隶书

楷书

草书

行书

简化字

（同楷书）

290

# 乳 rǔ

乳 in oracle bone inscriptions was genuinely an art masterpiece. Only with several strokes was the scene, i.e. the mother is milking the baby, finely depicted, even including the details. The initial meaning was "to give birth to a child." It also indicates "breasts," "milk," "to milk," etc.

甲骨文

秦简文

小篆

隶书

楷书

草书

行书

简化字

（同楷书）

# 弱 ruò

In ancient scripts, there existed a character, 弜. It was like two bows placed together, meaning 强, unyielding, pronounced jiàng. Therefore, if the bowstrings (represented by several slanting lines) already came loose, the meaning must have been "weak." The initial meaning was "poor," "thin and slender." It extended to indicate "slender," "to weaken," "to downfall," and so on.

（缺）

（缺）

（同楷书）

甲骨文

金文

小篆

隶书

楷书

草书

行书

简化字

292

# 散 sàn, sǎn

It was originally constituted of 林 (pài, 麻, not 林) and 攴 (pū, slight strike or hit). Its grapheme in bronze inscriptions appeared to be a hand softly striking hemp pieces with a stick in order to get them loose. The character was also added 月 as a radical to indicate evening laboring. Its original meanings were 分离, separating, 分散, dispersing, against that of 聚, gathering.

甲骨文

金文

小篆

隶书

楷书

草书

行书

简化字

（同楷书）

293

# 瑟 sè

瑟 was a kind of ancient plucked musical instrument. It looked like the shape of 古琴 (ancient harp) with twenty-five strings commonly. 瑟, with 琴 together, was called 琴瑟. Its middle form of 大 or 人 indicated the body, the horizontal line indicated the strings, and afterwards the radical 必 was added to indicate sound. (See character 琴.)

（缺）

甲骨文

说文『古文』

小篆

隶书

楷书

草书

行书

简化字

（同楷书）

294

# 森 sēn

The character is made up of three 木, symbolizing many trees. It extends to signify "many," "dense." It also means 阴暗, shady and dark.

（缺）

（同楷书）

# 杀（殺）shā

A beast's head was shot or hit by a sharp tool, and it was killed with its tail drooped. This scene was the ideograph of 杀 in oracle bone inscriptions. After small seal characters, another semantic symbol 殳 (weapon) was added. The original meaning is "to kill."

沙 shā

The primitive form was written as 少（see character 少）. Later，水 was added to form 沙，sand. It extended to mean 沙滩，beach，沙漠，desert，and so on.

甲骨文

金文

小篆

隶书

楷书

草书

行书

简化字

（同楷书）

# 膻（羴羶）shān

It was initially written as 羴. The original meaning referred to the odor of sheep or goats. In oracle bone inscriptions, its grapheme was the constitution of two to four 羊, signifying the strong smell of such an odor. Afterwards, a phonogram of 羶 was coined. In addition, there was another variant 膻, which originally meant 袒露, to expose. Today, 膻 is considered a standard version.

（缺）

| | |
|---|---|
| 甲骨文 | |
| 金文 | |
| 小篆 | |
| 隶书 | |
| 楷书 | |
| 草书 | |
| 行书 | |
| 简化字 | |

298

# 善 shàn

〔附〕膳 shàn

In oracle bone inscriptions, 善 was constituted of 羊 (i.e. 祥) and 目, symbolizing that something looked very nice. The lower part in bronze inscriptions changed into two 言, indicating two persons were talking in propitious words. It was interchangeable with 膳, food.

| | |
|---|---|
| | 甲骨文 |
| | 金文 |
| | 小篆 |
| | 隶书 |
| | 楷书 |
| | 草书 |
| | 行书 |
| | 简化字 |

（同楷书）

299

# 尚 shàng

Its original meaning was "to increase or add." It was made up of 八 (meaning to distribute things to others and have their property increased) and 向 (a sound symbol). It was interchangeable with 上.

# 勺 sháo

勺 was a spoon for the ancient people used to scoop liquor or wine. Its graph looked like a spoon, and the dot was the self-explanatory symbol indicating to be able to scoop something. In addition, it was used for a sacrificial term with the divination, i.e. 礿(yuè).

| 甲骨文 | 金文 | 小篆 | 隶书 | 楷书 | 草书 | 行书 | 简化字 |
|---|---|---|---|---|---|---|---|

（同楷书）

# 舍 (捨) shè, shě

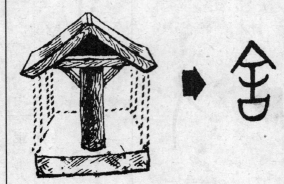

Its original meaning was 客馆, guest house. It was such a simple house that only a roof, a big column, a beam, and a foundation stone were needed for its denotation. When using in 舍弃, throw away, etc., it was pronounced shě, and afterwards written as 捨, which has been combined to 舍 again.

（缺）

甲骨文

金文
舍
舍

小篆
舍

隶书
舍

楷书
舍

草书
舍

行书
舍

简化字
（同楷书）

# 社 shè

The original meaning of the character was "the god of land." When using tortoise carapaces and mammal bones for divination, 土 was loaned to substitute for 社. Later, 社 became the basic-level administrative unit in local areas, i.e. "twenty-five families," or "the area of six square *li*," (three square kilometers).

（同楷书）

303

# 审（審）shěn

In a house （宀）, an animal's footprints were found （釆, not 采, see character 番）, so people one after another talked （口） to know what the matter it was. The initial meanings were 考察, to review or survey，研究, to study or investigate.

304

# 甚 shèn

The initial meaning was "too much free from worry." The upper part of the character in bronze inscriptions was 甘 (sweet); the lower a large spoon with food inside. Later, it extended to convey the meanings of 厉害, strict or rigorous, 过分, excessive, 超过, superior to, 很, very, etc.

（缺）

甲骨文

金文

小篆

隶书

楷书

草书

行书

简化字

（同楷书）

# 声（聲）shēng

Seen from the grapheme of oracle bone inscriptions, 声 was really a very "busy and lively" character: one hand was taking a little hammer and striking an ancient musical instrument 磬 (see character 磬); one mouth was singing; one ear was enclosed in the middle attentively listening to these voices.

甲骨文

（缺）

金文

小篆

隶书

楷书

草书

行书

简化字

# 牲 shēng

Its initial meaning was "the whole ox which was used for the sacrifice offering ceremony." 生 was a phonetic symbol; the earliest grapheme was formed of 羊 because the radicals of animals and livestock in oracle bone inscriptions were often exchanged one another; after bronze inscriptions the radical was fixed to be 牛. Later, it extensively referred to various sacrificial and edible livestock.

| | |
|---|---|
| 甲骨文 | |
| 金文 | |
| 小篆 | |
| 隶书 | |
| 楷书 | |
| 草书 | |
| 行书 | |
| 简化字 | （同楷书） |

# 师 (師) shī

甲骨文

金文

小篆

隶书

楷书

草书

行书

简化字

The original meaning was "army." Due to the fact the army often stationed on the hills, hence, 自（the same as 堆, low and small hill）in oracle bone inscriptions and bronze inscriptions was mostly loaned for 师. And in bronze inscriptions, it also had 帀（the same as 匝, to make a circuit）to indicate 师, and 師 were already appeared. In *Suo Wen*, two thousand and five hundred soldiers was named 师.

# 失 shī

From the grapheme of the Warring States Period scripts, it can be seen that an object was dropping under a hand. The original meaning was "to lose." Otherwise, the subsequent various variant forms are hard to trace their origins.

（缺）

（同楷书）

甲骨文 战国文字 小篆 隶书 楷书 草书 行书 简化字

309

# 湿（溼 濕）shī

Its initial meaning was "wet." Graphically in oracle bone inscriptions and bronze inscriptions, it was like "the silk being sunned with the water nearby." After small seal characters, it began to have 土 as a radical to form 溼. Since official script of the Han Dynasty, it was mostly written as 濕, and there was no difference between these two characters. The simplified version is 湿.

甲骨文

金文

小篆

隶书

楷书

草书

行书

简化字

310

# 实（實）shí

Its form of bronze inscriptions was made up of 宀 (house), 田 (field) and 贝 (wealth, ancient people regarded 贝 as currency), meaning "wealthy." After small seal characters, 田 and 贝 evolved into 贯, which is also understandable.

甲骨文

金文

小篆

隶书

楷书

草书

行书

简化字

311

# 世 shì

〔附〕叶（葉）yè

世 was the primitive form of 葉 （叶）. The grapheme in bronze inscriptions was several tree leaves linking together. Because year after year the autumn leaves fall and the spring leaves burgeon, just like man's life, hence, the character can be used figuratively. There was an old saying that "thirty years were called 一世（a generation），" or "after the father having a son also a generation."

| | |
|---|---|
| 甲骨文 | （缺） |
| 金文 | 业 |
| 小篆 | 世 |
| 隶书 | 世 |
| 楷书 | 世 |
| 草书 | 乞 |
| 行书 | 丝 |
| 简化字 | （同楷书） |

312

# 是 shì

The original meaning was "upright," "straight." Graphically in bronze inscriptions, the upper part looked like a sundial (some graph with a hand holding it); the lower part originally was 止 (subsequently changed to 正), indicating to walk following the correct direction.

313

# 士 shì

〔附〕仕 shì

The appellation to 士 experienced many changes. According to ancient books, as early as the Five Lords Period, it meant the punishment official of running the prisons. However in bronze inscriptions, its graph certainly looked like a large axe, which was a symbol for the punishment officials. It was also interchangeable with 仕, meaning 做官, being an official.

（同楷书）

314

# 视（視）shì

In many Chinese characters, 示 is often used as a radical (a semantic symbol). But in this one it is a phonetic radical (a sound symbol). The original meaning is "to see or look." It extends to signify 审查, censor, 看待, look on, etc.

# 筮 shì

Ancient people used 蓍草 to determine auspicious or ominous in divination. In bronze inscriptions, the middle part of 筮 was 巫, which was a bamboo prop for a necromancer to divine, so the upper part was 竹 and the bottom two hands.

（缺）

（同楷书）

# 收 shōu

收 originally meant 逮捕, to arrest, 拘押, to take into custody. It was constituted of 攴 (pū, meaning "to jump and attack," like a man hitting another with a stick, a semantic symbol) and 丩 (i.e. 纠, a phonetic symbol).

（缺）

甲骨文

三体石经

小篆

隶书

楷书

草书

行书

简化字

（同楷书）

# 手 shǒu

In bronze inscriptions, 手 graphically looked like a hand, and it was not a drawing but "very symbolic." It extends to indicate "craft," "by oneself," "a man specializing in a certain craft or a field," etc.

（缺）

甲骨文

金文

小篆

隶书

楷书

草书

行书

简化字

（同楷书）

318

# 守 shǒu

Its original meaning was "to protect," "to defend." 宀 indicated a house; 寸 or 又 indicated a hand. This is an associate compound character. It extends to mean 掌管, charge, 保持, keep, 遵行, follow, 等候, wait for, 节操, moral integrity, and others.

（缺）

（同楷书）

# 寿（壽）shòu

This character has many variants in ancient and modern times, but its basic construction was of 老 (indicating its meaning) and 弖 (i.e. 疇, indicating its sound. See character 疇). The original meaning was "aging." Its extended meanings are 长寿, longevity, 寿命, life-span, 生日, birthday, and so on.

320

# 书（書）shū

It is a phonogram, constituted of 聿 (笔) as a pictographic radical (a semantic symbol) and 者 (its primitive sound like that of 诸) as a phonetic radical (a phonetic symbol). Its original meaning was "to write down," "to record in writing." It extended to mean "writings or books," "written language," "handwritings," "letters," etc.

# 叔 shū

Its initial meaning was 拾取, to pick up. In bronze inscriptions its graph seemed to be a hand picking up beans under a beanstalk（see character 菽）. Later, it was loaned to be 叔（see character 吊 for reference to its another form）of 叔伯.

甲骨文

金文

叔

小篆

叔

隶书

叔

楷书

叔

草书

村

行书

叔

简化字

（同楷书）

322

# 菽 shū

The original form was written as 尗, like a bean bud sprouting out of the earth. It is the general term for all the beans or leguminous plants. Today, it is written as 菽.

（缺）

甲骨文

金文

小篆

隶书

楷书

草书

行书

简化字

（同楷书）

323

# 殳 shū

It was the name for an ancient weapon, made of bamboo or wood. It was one 丈 two 尺 (almost four meters) long, with edge but no blade on its top. It was also written as 杸.

甲骨文
金文
小篆
隶书
楷书
草书
行书
简化字

（同楷书）

324

# 孰 shú

〔附〕熟 shú

It was the original form of 熟. Graphically in oracle bone inscriptions, it was a man in front of a clan temple offering cooked food to ancestors. In bronze inscriptions, the lower part 女 of 享 was one from the wrong change of 夂 (the shape of man's foot). Later, it was mostly loaned to use as a pronoun, so 火 was added to invent another character 熟.

（同楷书）

# 鼠 shǔ

In oracle bone inscriptions, it was really a vividly delineated pictograph: extruding mouth, sharp teeth, arched back, short legs, long tail, and some food leftovers nearby. In *Suo Wen*, it referred to all animals living in caves.

| |
| --- |
| 甲骨文 |
| 金文 |
| 小篆 |
| 隶书 |
| 楷书 |
| 草书 |
| 行书 |
| 简化字 |

（同楷书）

326

# 树（樹）shù

The original meaning was "to seed," "to plant." The earliest graphemes we could see were all that a seedling was being planted with a hand to hold it, and 豆 was used to indicate sound. It is also the general term for wood plants.

# 庶 shù

〔附〕煮 zhǔ

It was the original form of 煮. Its form graphically was a pan（口）under the mountain cliff（厂）and the fire （火）below the pan was burning the food. Later, 厂 mistakenly changed to 广, 口 changed to 廿, and 火 changed to 灬, which could not be explained in reason. It also means "many or plenty of," "fertile," etc.

甲骨文

金文

小篆

隶书

楷书

草书

行书

简化字

（同楷书）

328

# 衰 shuāi

〔附〕蓑 suō

It was the original meaning of 蓑 (suō). This is an ideograph and its initial form was like a raincoat knotted by grass, palm leaves or tree leaves. Later, with its original meaning not in use frequently, it was mostly loaned to indicate "decline," "decadency," "ebb," and others.

金文

小篆

隶书

楷书

草书

行书

简化字

（同楷书）

# 帅（帥）shuài

〔附〕帨 shuì

The original meaning was "an cloth ornament." Its graph in oracle bone inscriptions was a pair of hands taking a cleaning towel（its side shape）. In bronze inscriptions it began to add the radical 巾. Later，帅 was mostly to indicate 统帅，commanding，率领，leading，hence another character 帨 was invented.

| 甲骨文 |
| 金文 |
| 小篆 |
| 隶书 |
| 楷书 |
| 草书 |
| 行书 |
| 简化字 |

# 双（雙）shuāng

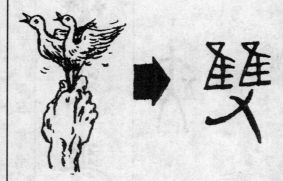

One bird（隹）caught by one hand is 隻（the same as 獲［获］）；two birds caught by one hand is 雙（双）. Its initial meaning was "two birds." Subsequently, it extensively refers to "a pair" of other things.

战国文字　雙

小篆　雙

隶书　雙

楷书　雙

草书　雙

行书　双

简化字　双

# 爽 shuǎng

Its original meaning was "bright." Graphically in oracle bone inscriptions, it was like an upstanding person with fire pans or lamps on both sides. Due to its much change in forms later on, it is difficult to trace its original significance. 昧爽, i.e. 早晨, morning.

甲骨文

金文

小篆

隶书

楷书

草书

行书

简化字

（同楷书）

# 顺（順）shùn

This is a phonogram: 页 is man's head, signifying its meaning; 巛, i.e. 川, as well as 𩠐 (shùn, the dropped hair when combing), signifies its sound. Its initial meaning is 顺从, obey, 顺应, conformance.

# 硕（碩）shuò

It originally meant "big head." 页 is man's head; 石 indicates its sound. It extends to indicate "big" of other things.

甲骨文

金文

小篆

隶书

楷书

草书

行书

简化字

334

# 思 SĪ

The upper part of the character was not 田 but 囟 (囟门, indicating man's brain. See character 囟); the lower part was 心. The ancient people thought brains and hearts were both thinking organs. Its original meaning was 思考, "to think."

（同楷书）

335

# 私 SĪ

私 in 自私 was originally written as ㄙ, which meant 奸邪, "crafty and fawning." Since small seal characters, the character 私 began to emerge, which originally had been the name for grains or cereals.

336

# 斯 sī

The original meaning was 劈开, to split, which was composed of 斤 and 其 as a sound symbol. 斤 was just an ax. It extended to signify "to disperse," "to leave," "to tear up," etc. It was also used as a function word.

甲骨文

（缺）

金文

斯

小篆

斯

隶书

其斤

楷书

斯

草书

斱

行书

斯

简化字

（同楷书）

寺 **sì**

〔附〕持 chí 恃 shì

It was both the original form and meaning of 持. Later, it was loaned to indicate the title for a governmental office, and it mostly referred to the temples of Buddhism. In addition, it was interchangeable with 恃.

（缺）

甲骨文

金文

小篆

隶书

楷书

草书

行书

简化字

（同楷书）

338

# 嗣 sì

Its original meaning was "to ascend the throne of emperors or kings." As a rule, emperors or kings usually ascended the throne to their eldest son, therefore, in oracle bone inscriptions, the character was composed of 册, 大, and 子, meaning to accede the eldest son to the throne. In bronze inscriptions, it changed to the constitution of 口, 册 and 司 (as a phonetic symbol).

（同楷书）

# 巳 sì

Its original meaning was "fetus." Its graph looked like a fetus in the mother's belly of a very big head and a bent body. However, the fetus's head was upwards and it was not the factual case. Later, it was loaned to indicate the sixth of the Earthly Branches and it could count year, month, day, and hour.

（同楷书）

# 兕 sì

In ancient times, the character of 兕 referred to rhinoceros. It was also written as 㺉, which was just like a wild ox but of the blue color, and also very pictographic.

（同楷书）

# 送 sòng

It was initially made up of 㚀, kindling, 彳 and 止 (later 彳 and 止 evolved into 辵, indicating action). The primitive people especially cherish kindling, so they sent it to others for a profound friendship.

（缺）

（同楷书）

# 宋 sòng

It initially meant "to dwell on." In order to live in peace and contentment, people had to build houses and make furniture with wood. Therefore, in a house (宀) was stored some wood (木) (also regarded as the elide pronunciation of 松). With its original significance not existent any more, it was mostly loaned for a special term.

甲骨文

金文

小篆

隶书

楷书

草书

行书

简化字

（同楷书）

# 叟 sǒu

〔附〕搜 sōu

It was the original form of 搜, and also written as 变. Graphically in oracle bone inscriptions, it took the likeness of a hand raising a touch and looking for something in the house. In ancient books, it was loaned to address elderly males.

（同楷书）

344

# 素 sù

Its original meaning was "the crude silk of primitive color." The crude silk is thick and often droopy, so such a characteristic was clearly signified by the upper part of the character in both bronze inscriptions and small seal characters. It extended to mean 本色, primitive color, 白色, white color, 本质, essence, 质朴, plain and simple, etc.

# 粟 sù

It extensively referred to cereals or grains in ancient times. In the later days, the character especially indicated the fillet.

<table>
<tr><td>甲骨文</td></tr>
<tr><td>籀文</td></tr>
<tr><td>小篆</td></tr>
<tr><td>隶书</td></tr>
<tr><td>楷书</td></tr>
<tr><td>草书</td></tr>
<tr><td>行书</td></tr>
<tr><td>简化字</td></tr>
</table>

（同楷书）

# 肃（肅）sù

It was composed of 聿 and 片, i.e. 聿 on the top of 片, meaning "gingerly." The former was 笔, signifying to act or work, and the latter was 渊. The meaning of 肃 is: anything should be done solemnly and cautiously, as if walking by the edge of a deep pool.

# 虽（雖）suī

佳 was loaned to be a pictographic radical（a meaning symbol）of birds to form many characters. But in 雖（虽）, it was only used as a phonetic radical（a sound symbol）to indicate the animal of another kind — 大蜥蜴, enormous lizards. Subsequently, it was mostly loaned to be a function word.

（缺）

甲骨文

金文 雖

小篆 雖

隶书 雖

楷书 雖

草书 雖

行书 雖

简化字 虽

# 所 suǒ

所 is made up of 户 (a phonetic radical) and 斤 (a graphic radical). The original meaning was "the sound produced during lumbering." Later, it was loaned to indicate "a living place," etc. and also a function word.

# 它（牠）tā

〔附〕蛇 shé

它 was the original form and meaning of 蛇, snake. Subsequently, it was often loaned to use as a pronoun. In simplified characters, 它 and 牠 are both combined to 它.

| 甲骨文 |
| 金文 |
| 小篆 |
| 隶书 |
| 楷书 |
| 草书 |
| 行书 |
| 简化字 |

（同楷书）

# 台 (臺檯颱) tái

〔附〕怡 yí

This five-stroke character actually turns out to be a phonogram: 口 indicates its meaning and 目 (i.e. 以, see character 以) indicates its sound. 台 was the original form of 怡. In simplified characters, 臺, 檯 and 颱 are all combined to 台.

（缺）

（同楷书）

# 泰 tài

〔附〕汏 tài 汰 dà 太 tài

Its initial meaning was "to cleanse or wash." It was interchangeable with 汏 and 汰. Its form was like a hand washing something on the water, of which the upper part 大 was as a phonetic symbol. In ancient writings, it was mostly loaned to signify "extend in all directions," "safety and peace," "good and fine," "wealth and richness," "immense," etc. It was also interchangeable with 太. Sometimes it was written as 太.

甲骨文

（缺）

说文『古文』

小篆

隶书

楷书

草书

（同楷书）

行书

简化字

352

堂 táng

Its original meaning was "the man-made square earthly terrace," i.e. 坛（壇）, altar. The character was composed of 土 and 尚 (as a phonetic symbol, but its form was simplified to some extent). It also referred to "house foundation." Later, people also name 殿, palace, as 堂.

甲骨文

（缺）

金文

小篆

隶书

楷书

草书

行书

简化字

（同楷书）

353

# 唐 táng

唐 is a phonogram: 口 indicates its meaning and 庚 indicates its sound. Its original meaning was "to talk tall." It extends to mean 广大, vastness.

（同楷书）

354

# 陶 táo

It was originally written as 匋. Graphically in bronze inscriptions, it was like a man with his bent body and his extended hand making the tile crockery with a pestle. It originally meant "the tile crockery." Later, 阜（left 阝）was added to signify digging clay from the hill for crockery making. It extended to mean 化育, cultivate and convert, 培养, bring up, 喜悦, happiness, etc.

（缺）

甲骨文

金文

小篆

隶书

楷书

草书

行书

简化字

（同楷书）

# 惕 tì

甲骨文

金文

小篆

隶书

楷书

草书

行书

简化字

（同楷书）

The character was made up of 心 (indicating its significance) and 易 (indicating its sound). Its original meaning was 警惕, on guard, 戒惧, guard and cautious. It also had the meanings of 恭敬, respectful, 忧伤, sorrow and grief, etc.

# 替 tì

It originally meant 松弛, relaxation，懈怠，keep a slack hand. Its graph in bronze inscriptions was like two persons yawning with their mouths widely extruded, signifying to be very tired and fatigue. It extended to take on the meanings of 废弃，abandon，衰败，decline and decay, and 更代，replace or substitute for, etc.

357

# 亭 tíng

〔附〕停 tíng

Its constitution was of 高 (indicating meaning but with its form simplified) and 丁 (indicating sound). The original meaning was a house where visitors or guests could stay or rest by the road. It was interchangeable with 停.

甲骨文 (缺)

古陶文 高

小篆 高

隶书 亭

楷书 亭

草书 亭

行书 亭

简化字 (同楷书)

358

# 廷 tíng

〔附〕庭 tíng

It was the original form of 庭. Its original meaning was 庭院, courtyard. Its grapheme was like a man who was carrying the earth and the stones with his body bent and working in front of the foundation ground of a construction. It extended to indicate 朝廷, the court, 官署, governmental office, etc.

（缺）

甲骨文

金文

小篆

隶书

楷书

草书

行书

简化字

（同楷书）

# 童（僮）tóng

〔附〕瞳 tóng

Its initial meaning was "man slaves." The early grapheme in bronze inscriptions was made up of two parts, the upper one like a punishment knife (see character 辛) stabbing a man's eye and made him slave; the lower part 东, indicating sound. Later, 童 mostly referred to "children," so another character 僮 was coined to express the initial significance. It was interchangeable with 瞳, pupil of the eye, e.g. 童(瞳)子.

（缺）

（同楷书）

360

# 彤 tóng

Its meaning is "to coat or paint with red color." It is made up of 丹（硃砂, red color）and 彡（the symbol for brilliance）. It still takes on the meaning of 赤红色, crimson.

彤

彤

彤

彤

彤

彤

（同楷书）

361

# 突 tū

A dog suddenly run out of the cave and began to bite a person, which was really an unexpected matter. Its meaning is 突然, sudden. It again contains the meaning of 冲撞, collide. Today, 突围, break through, is still in use.

突
窔
窔
突
窔
窔

（同楷书）

362

# 图（圖）tú

Its initial meaning is "atlas or map." □ represents the map frame; 啚, i.e. 鄙, means the remote area. With the remotest place or area included certainly means the territory of a state or a country.

363

# 退 tuì

（缺）

The character was constituted of 彳, 日 and 夂. The radical of 彳, the same significance as 辵, indicated action; 日, indicated time; 夂 was the converse written form of 止 (趾, foot), taking on the meaning of backing off and descending. The three forms joined together indicated it was time to go back. The original meanings were "receding," "leaving," "returning."

甲骨文

金文

小篆

隶书

楷书

草书

行书

简化字

（同楷书）

364

# 瓦 wǎ

The earthenware before being fired is called 坯, and after that is named 瓦. It also refers to "house tiles." It furthermore refers to "spindles fired by the clay."

365

# 外 wài

外 is constituted of 夕 (in ancient times 月 and 夕 were the same one character) and 卜, to divine. The divination was usually done during the daytime, but if done during the evening time, it would be the case of "exceptional," or "additional." It extended to be 疏远, alienation, 背离, deviation, 排斥, exclude, 外表, appearance, etc.

卟 卟 外 外 外

（同楷书）

366

# 微 wēi

The character was originally written as 散, which was like a person combing hair with a comb. Human being's hair is fine and beautiful, so its initial meaning was 妙, fine and wonderful. It was also the original form of 媺（the same as 美）. Later, the character was added 彳 as a radical and it mostly meant "tiny."

（同楷书）

# 威 wēi

A little weak woman must feel terribly deterred when she faced a huge weapon（戌）in front of her. Its initial meaning was "to frighten." It extended to indicate 威力, power, and 权势, power and influence.

甲骨文

金文

小篆

隶书

楷书

草书

行书

简化字

（缺）

（同楷书）

# 危 wēi

When a horse cart went wrong, a person suddenly caught hold of the yoke and got it halt. Actually, 危 in small seal characters was just made up of 人 and 厄（see character 厄）. Its initial meaning is "in danger," "insecurity."

（缺）

（同楷书）

甲骨文

战国文字

小篆

隶书

楷书

草书

行书

简化字

# 委 wěi

〔附〕萎 wěi

A woman kneeling down by a with-ering curve stalk was much symbolic in meaning: the woman had yielded to an-other wrongly and reluctantly. It extends to indicate "subordinate to," "entrust with," "abandon," "shift off," etc. It was also interchangeable with 萎.

甲骨文

金文

小篆

隶书

楷书

草书

行书

简化字

（同楷书）

370

# 胃 wèi

〔附〕谓（謂）wèi

The upper part of the character is the form of 胃, stomach, which had a pointed shape at the top in bronze inscriptions and had dots inside to signify food in small seal characters; the lower part is 月, i.e. 肉, indicating this is a body organ. It was interchangeable with 谓.

（缺）

（同楷书）

卧 wò

（缺）

Awaken or asleep, which can be obviously noticed by the change of eyes, therefore, 卧 is just represented by 臣 （i.e. the shape of 目, eyes）and 卜 （the variant of 人）. Its initial meaning was "fall asleep," or "rest with eyes closed."

甲骨文

金文

小篆

隶书

楷书

草书

行书

简化字

（同楷书）

372

# 乌（烏）wū

〔附〕於 yú, yū, wū

The original meaning is 乌鸦, crow. The difference between 乌 and 鸟 is, the latter has an "eye" and the former doesn't have (but in bronze inscriptions some particular items were exceptional). This is because crows are completely black and their eyes can not be seen. It extends to signify "black color." It was interchangeable with 於 in ancient times.

373

# 兮 XĪ

The lower part is 丂 (the original form of 柯, axe handle), signifying its pronunciation; the upper is two vertical strokes, signifying the rising of the voice. It was often loaned to function as tone of expression; when used in rhyme writings（韵文）it was identical to 啊.（See character 乎.）

（同楷书）

# 悉 XĪ

Its upper part is the footprints of animals (釆, see character 番); its lower part is 心, which means that you understand the present situation within yourself. Its original meaning was 详尽, full and clear, such as 知悉, to know, 洞悉, to discern, 获悉, to learn, etc. It also contains the significance of 尽, "all," 全部, "whole."

| 甲骨文 | （缺） |
|---|---|
| 战国文字 | |
| 小篆 | |
| 隶书 | |
| 楷书 | |
| 草书 | |
| 行书 | |
| 简化字 | （同楷书） |

息 XĪ

Composed of 心 and 自（also indicating its pronunciation）, it meant "breathing." The original meaning was "flatus." It extended to mean "sighing," "resting," and so on.

甲骨文 （缺）

金文

小篆

隶书

楷书

草书

行书

简化字 （同楷书）

376

# 席（蓆）xí

Its initial meaning was 席子, matting. The earlier grapheme appeared to be a mat with some weaving lines on it. Later, it extended to indicate 席位, seat，职务, position, 酒席, feast, etc. Today, its variant 蓆 has been combined to 席.

（同楷书）

徙 xǐ

It originally meant 迁移, move or migrate. Graphically in bronze inscriptions, it was like a pair of feet alone the path（彳, the simplified form of 行）walking ahead. It extended to mean "transfer to a new position," "exile," etc.

（同楷书）

| | |
|---|---|
| 甲骨文 | |
| 金文 | |
| 小篆 | |
| 隶书 | |
| 楷书 | |
| 草书 | |
| 行书 | |
| 简化字 | |

# 夏 xià

Its original meaning was "the people of Chinese," i.e. the name for an ancient tribe living in the Central Plains of China. Today, the Chinese people still name themselves 华夏. In bronze inscriptions, its graph was like a head and a man with both hands and feet. 夏 of 夏天 is a homophonic loan character.

（缺）

甲骨文

金文

小篆

隶书

楷书

草书

行书

简化字

夏 夏 夏 夏 夏

（同楷书）

379

# 鲜（鮮）xiān , xiǎn

鲜 was the name of a fish original-ly, of which the radical 羊 was the sim-plified form of 羴（shān, see character 膻）and also indicated sound. Later, the character extensively referred to "living fish." Its extended meanings were "fresh," "delicious food," "good and kind," "bright," etc. In addition, it had the meaning of 少, a little, pro-nounced xiǎn.

# 涎 xián

It was initially written as 次（not 次）. Its grapheme looked like a man with his widely open mouth drooling the long dribbles.（See characters 羡，盗.）In modern Chinese, there is an idiom, 垂涎三尺, to spittle three feet long, i.e. to drool with envy.

（同楷书）

381

# 闲（閑閒）xián

The original meaning was "wooden railing." It was made up of 门, door, and 木, wood. Its extended meaning was 马厩, stable. Later, 閑 and 閒 were once exchangeable in use for some time. Their simplified versions are combined to 闲.

（缺）

甲骨文

金文

小篆

隶书

楷书

草书

行书

简化字

# 贤（賢）xián

It was initially written as 臤. Its earlier grapheme was like a submitting eye with a capable hand which was considered a "good" slave. Its original meaning was "good," "kind." It also meant "tired," or "overworked." Later, the radical 贝 was added to indicate "much wealth."

| | |
|---|---|
| 甲骨文 | 臤 |
| 金文 | 臤 賢 |
| 小篆 | 賢 |
| 隶书 | 賢 |
| 楷书 | 賢 |
| 草书 | 贤 |
| 行书 | 贤 |
| 简化字 | 贤 |

# 显（顯）xiǎn

A person was under the sun watching the silk, and the silk was so thin that it could be only seen clearly in the sun. Its original meaning was 明显, clear and obvious. Its extended meanings were 显扬, to show off, and others.

（缺）

甲骨文

金文

小篆

隶书

楷书

草书

行书

简化字

384

# 限 xiàn

A man wanted to turn round to see further, but a hill stopped his sight. It initially indicated the meaning of "to stop" or "to prevent." It extended to indicate "confine," "limit," "dividing line," "end," and "doorsill," etc.

（同楷书）

# 县（縣）xiàn

〔附〕悬（懸）xuán

It was a cruel picture: a person's head tied by the rope was hanging from a tree. The character 县 was just the original form of 悬, meaning "to hang." Later, it was loaned mostly to be the name for an administrative unit, i.e. county.

甲骨文

（缺）

金文

小篆

隶书

楷书

草书

行书

简化字

# 宪（憲）xiàn

It was the initial form of 幰 (pronounced xiǎn nowadays). It meant "the curtain of a carriage or a cart," which was used to prevent the sunshine or resisted the hot. 憲 in bronze inscriptions didn't have 心 mostly but the form of an umbrella-shape and an eye (representing the face) together. In ancient books, 憲 meant 敏, agile. Subsequently, it mostly indicated 法令, legal order, 典范, apotheosis, etc.

# 羨 xiàn

Its upper part was 羊; the lower part was 次 (see character 涎), i.e. a person was drooling. Therefore, the whole meaning was "to covet to the mutton." The original significance was "be fond of," or "to lust for obtaining."

甲骨文 （缺）

金文 （缺）

小篆 羊涎

隶书 羡

楷书 羡

草书 羡

行书 羡

简化字 （同楷书）

388

# 香 xiāng

It was made up of 黍（glutinous millet）and 甘（甜）, signifying such a grain was sweet and delicious. Its initial meaning was "fragrant smell," or "sweetness."

（同楷书）

# 祥 xiáng

The ancient people often substituted 羊 for 祥. Later, the radical 示 (sacrificial table) was added to indicate its significance. It originally meant "happy," "lucky," "fine."

甲骨文

金文

小篆

隶书

楷书

草书

行书

简化字

（同楷书）

390

# 枭（梟）xiāo

〔附〕鸮（鴞）xiāo

枭 refers to a general term for all the birds of 鸱鸮 family, also written as 鸮, colloquially namely 猫头鹰, owl. This kind of birds was often thought of "impious birds," or "wicked birds." Hence，枭雄 indicates tough and ambitious persons；枭首 indicates that the beheaded head was hung on the tree for show to warn others.

甲骨文

金文

小篆

隶书

楷书

草书

行书

简化字

（缺）

# 嚣（囂）xiāo

It originally meant 喧哗, noisy and roaring. The middle of the character is 页, man's head, and there were four 口 beside, emphasizing the noisy sound.

# 协（協）xié

〔附〕叶 xié

It was originally written as 劦. The grapheme in oracle bone inscriptions was three 力, showing that many people were laboring together. Later, it was written as 協 or 恊, and also as 叶. The initial meaning was "together." It extended to mean "harmony," "coincidence," etc. In the simplified versions, 叶 is used to substitute for 葉, but as 叶韵 it is still pronounced xié.

# 写（寫）xiě

It was made up of 宀 and 舄（indicating sound）. It originally meant "to place things in a house," or "put." Later, it was mostly loaned to indicate "writing." 舄（xì）, i.e. magpie, also referred to shoes with the wooden soles added, but here just as a phonetic symbol.

甲骨文
石鼓文
小篆
隶书
楷书
草书
行书
简化字

寫
寫
寫
宁
寫
写

394

# 燮 xiè

A hand was taking an animal's leg or this kind of food and then got it burned on several fires, which was certainly burned well down and delicious. Later, the food form mistakenly became 言 or 辛, hence, two characters were invented. The former 燮 meant 和, and the latter 爕 meant "well done cooked." In fact, they were variants of the same character.

（同楷书）

# 信 xìn

〔附〕伸 shēn

信 was made up of 人 and 言, an associate compound character. But in bronze inscriptions, there was also a form of 人 and 口. It initially meant "honesty." The extended meanings were "believe," "trust in," "believe in," "conform," "news," "letters," etc. It was interchangeable with 伸.

（缺）

（同楷书）

甲骨文

金文

小篆

隶书

楷书

草书

行书

简化字

# 囟 xìn

As a pictograph, it originally meant 囟门, fontanel, which is on the central part of the head top, i. e. the place that hasn't been already closed to a baby. The upper part of 思 was once written as 囟.

| | |
|---|---|
| 甲骨文 | ⊕ |
| 金文 | ⊕ |
| 小篆 | 囟 |
| 隶书 | 卤 |
| 楷书 | 囟 |
| 草书 | （缺） |
| 行书 | |
| 简化字 | 囟 （同楷书） |

# 刑 xíng

It was primitively constituted of 刀 and 井 (as a sound symbol). In ancient times, in order to maintain the order for civilians to get water out of the well, the local feudal official once sent soldiers with knives to guard the well in case disputes would be arisen. Its original meaning was "to punish and bring under control." It extended to indicate 法律, law.

（缺）

甲骨文

金文

小篆

隶书

楷书

草书

行书

简化字

（同楷书）

398

# 幸 xìng

幸 originated from the combination of two different characters in significance and pronunciation: 㚔 (niè) and 夭 (xìng). The former meant "handcuff," and the latter "being propitious but ominous." Subsequently, the former was written as 𣕕 (niè); the latter was only used to refer to 幸 (xìng) in 幸运, lucky, and 幸福, happy.

甲骨文

金文

小篆

隶书

楷书

草书

行书

简化字

（同楷书）

399

# 凶（兇）xiōng

The earth collapsed and the big delve was full of stakes and thorns, which certainly was a terrible matter. Its initial meaning was "unlucky," or "misfortune." The extended meanings were "vicious," "outrageous," "wicked persons," etc. Its variant version was 兇, and combined to 凶 today.

（缺）

（同楷书）

400

秀 xiù

Its original meaning was "tassel and blossom of cereal crops," or "seeding of grass." It extended to indicate "flower or blossom," "flourish," "excellent," "pretty," etc.

（缺）

甲骨文

石鼓文

小篆

隶书

楷书

草书

行书

简化字

（同楷书）

401

# 须 (須鬚) xū

It was the original form of 鬚. Graphically in oracle bone inscriptions, it was several pieces of hair under one's mouth. However, in bronze inscriptions, the upper part of the character was a head-shape. And after small seal characters, its head form became 頁.

甲骨文

金文

小篆

隶书

楷书

草书

行书

简化字

402

# 虚 xū

〔附〕墟 xū

It was composed of 虍 (tiger's head, a phonetic symbol) and 丘 (a semantic symbol). 虚, meant 大丘, a large mound. It was interchangeable with 墟, ruins. The extended meanings are "emptiness," "scarce," "short of," "illusive," "coward," etc.

# 玄 xuán

〔附〕弦 xián

It was the initial form of 弦. The primitive character looked like a bow-string plaited by a piece of leather. With the color of leather it was often loaned to mean "reddish black color." It again takes on the meanings of "far-reaching," "cabalistic."

# 穴 xué

Its original meaning is "grotto." The character was not seen in oracle bone inscriptions or bronze inscriptions, but its original grapheme might be traced back from the characters with the radical of 穴.

（同楷书）

405

# 学（學）xué

It meant 学校, school, initially. The character in oracle bone inscriptions was a house, on which 爻 (indicating sound) was added; some other versions had a pair of hands symbolizing "together running the school." Since bronze inscriptions, it has been added 子 inside the house for the significance of cultivating learned children.

406

# 熏 (薰 燻) xūn

The grapheme in bronze inscriptions was like a chimney smoked and darkened by the fire: the form of 屮 indicated the rising smoke; 田 indicated the chimney being smoked and darkened; 火 was at the bottom. Its variant forms 薰 (also a name for sweet grass) and 燻 are combined to 熏 now.

（缺）

（同楷书）

407

# 牙 yá

〔附〕芽 yá

The character was not found in oracle bone inscriptions. In bronze inscriptions, it was like two animal teeth interlocked up and down. Its original meaning was "tooth," especially referring to ivory. In ancient writings, it was also used as 芽 of 草木萌芽, sprouting of grass and trees.

408

# 焉 yān

As a pictograph, the character looked like a long-tailed bird, and the form of 正 was the variant of the head feather. Later, it was loaned for use as an auxiliary word and the original sense was gone.

甲骨文

（缺）

金文

小篆

隶书

楷书

草书

行书

简化字

（同楷书）

409

# 延 yán

Its original meaning was "to walk." Primitively it was constituted of 彳 and 止. Subsequently, it evolved and diverged into 辿 (chān, walking slowly) and 延 (yán, walking for a long time). It also extended to mean 长久, lasting, 拖延, delay, 接待, receive, etc. As early as in oracle bone inscriptions, there had been the significance of 长 in divination of tortoise carapaces and mammal bones, such as 延多雨.

（同楷书）

410

# 岩 (巖) yán

The grapheme in oracle bone inscriptions seemed to be several rocks (口) on the hill. Its initial meaning was "peaks formed by the extruding rocks." It also refers to "lofty mountains." Its variant version was written as 岩. Nowadays, 岩 has already replaced 巖 in simplified characters.

| | |
|---|---|
| 甲骨文 | |
| 金文 | (缺) |
| 小篆 | |
| 隶书 | |
| 楷书 | |
| 草书 | |
| 行书 | |
| 简化字 | |

# 衍 yǎn

The character is constituted of 水 and 行, and its original meaning is "high tide." Its extended meanings are "rich in," "superabundance," "enlarge," "deduct and demonstrate," etc.

（同楷书）

# 厌（厭）yàn

〔附〕餍（饜）yàn

厌 was the primitive form of 餍. Its original meaning is "to eat one's fill," "content." The character was primitively written as 猒, composed of 犬，口 and 月（肉），signifying that a dog has been quite content with a large piece of meat in its mouth. It extends to indicate 厌恶, disgusted with, and so on.

# 燕 yàn, yān

〔附〕宴 yàn

Graphically in oracle bone inscriptions, it took the shape of a soaring swallow, whose typical characteristic was its scissors-like tail. It was interchangeable with 宴 when meaning 安闲, going easy, 饮宴, feast. As a proper term, it was pronounced yān. 燕, the name for an ancient state, had been originally written as 匽 or 郾.

甲骨文

金文

小篆

隶书

楷书

草书

行书

简化字

（同楷书）

414

# 雁（鴈）yàn

〔附〕赝（贋）yàn

雁 and 鴈 primitively differed with each other in meaning: the former referred to 鸿雁, swan goose, and the latter 鹅, goose. They were usually confused with their use, but today are combined to 雁. 厂 initially meant mountain cliff, indicating sound; a vertical stroke had been a variant version and later changed into 人 wrongly. It was also interchangeable with 赝, meaning "phony," "false."

（缺）

甲骨文

金文

小篆

隶书

楷书

草书

行书

简化字

（同楷书）

415

# 彦 yàn

It meant 贤士, i.e. an extraordinary person of talent and virtue. It was constituted of 文 (a semantic symbol, talent), 弓 (also a semantic symbol, martial strategy), and 厂 (hǎn, mountain cliff, representing sound). Subsequently, 弓 changed to 彡.

（缺）

（同楷书）

甲骨文

金文

小篆

隶书

楷书

草书

行书

简化字

416

# 仰 yǎng

It was originally written as 卬, of which one side was a proudly standing man and the other side a kneeling man with his head up for a hope. It meant "to raise the head and look up to." It extended to signify "adore," "rely on," etc.

甲骨文
金文
小篆
隶书
楷书
草书
行书
简化字

（同楷书）

417

# 爻 yáo

爻 was a denotation of divinatory symbols in *Yi Jing*, *Book of Changes*. The primitive grapheme was like several bamboo slips for divination placed staggered. According to the book, there were only two kinds of 爻: — meant 阳爻, and -- meant 阴爻; every three 爻 consisted of one 卦, and all together eight trigrams (八卦) were formed; if two 卦 were added together (i.e. six 爻), 64 hexagrams (六十四卦) were formed.

甲骨文

金文

小篆

隶书

楷书

草书

行书

简化字

（同楷书）

418

# 杳 yǎo

It is an associate compound character. When the sun was setting to the root of a tree, it meant that it was already in dusk. Its original meaning was "gloom." And its extended significance was "out of sight." Today, there are still idioms such as 杳无音信, never been heard of since; 杳如黄鹤, leave like the yellow crane, i.e. be gone for ever, etc.

甲骨文
古陶文
小篆
隶书
楷书
草书
行书
简化字

（同楷书）

419

# 夜 yè

The character was made up of 夕 (the same as 月 in ancient times) and 亦 (indicating the sound but simplified in form). The original meaning is "evening." It also refers to "dusk."

# 业（業）yè

It primitively referred to the horizontal board on the ancient musical rack, which was carved jaggedly to hang clocks, 磬, inverted bells, and others. Later, it also referred to the construction wallboards and book splints. Its extended meanings were 学业, schooling, 业务, profession, 职业, occupation, 产业, industry, 基业, a foundation for property, estate, etc.

# 叶 （葉）yè

葉 has been simplified to 叶 (the same as 协, xié, such as 叶韵). The original form of 葉 was written as 枼; later it was added 艸 as 葉. It extended to mean 书页, a page (e.g. 册葉 [叶]), something leave-like (e.g. 肺葉[叶], a piece of lung), etc.

422

# 依 yī

Composed of 人 and 衣 (indicating sound), its original meaning was "to rest on," "to lean against." The extended meaning was "to follow," "according to." It also referred to 顺从, submit to, 仍旧, still, etc.

甲骨文

金文

小篆

隶书

楷书

草书

行书

简化字

(缺)

(同楷书)

# 以 yǐ

〔附〕目 yǐ 已 yǐ

以 was also written as 目. It was the original form of 耜（sì）. 耜 was the bottom part of the ancient farm tool named 耒，which was used for shoving the earth. Just for its use as a farm tool，it was loaned to mean 用，use，使用，use. Later，it was mostly used as a function word. It was interchangeable with 已.

甲骨文

金文

小篆

隶书

楷书

草书

行书

简化字

（同楷书）

424

# 弋 yì

It meant "a stake" initially. Its grapheme was just like a piece of trunk with several branches and a horizontal board with nails for tying livestock and hanging objects. Subsequently, it indicated a short arrow with a string to its end.

甲骨文

金文

小篆

隶书

楷书

草书

行书

简化字

（同楷书）

425

# 意 yì

〔附〕忆(憶)yì

The character consisted of 心 and 音 (the same as 言 in ancient writings). Just as the expression says, words are the voice of the mind. It was interchangeable with 忆 (憶), remember or memory.

426

# 逸 yì

The original meaning is "to run away." Rabbits run very fast, hence, 兔 and 彳, 止 (later they were combined to 辵, indicating action) consisted of this character and its significance. The extended meanings were "fast running," "lose," "reclusion," "leisurely and comfortable," "indulgence," etc.

甲骨文

（缺）

金文

小篆

隶书

楷书

草书

行书

简化字

徙

趦

逸

逸

逸

逸

（同楷书）

427

# 肄 yì

Its original meaning was "laboring." The primitive grapheme in ancient scripts was like a hand (some with a piece of cloth) cleaning and washing domestic animals. It also has the meaning of "learning."

甲骨文

金文

小篆

隶书

楷书

草书

行书

简化字

（同楷书）

# 役 yì

Behind a man, a hand with a big stab was driving him to work. This was the original meaning of 役: being forced to take the penal servitude. It extended to mean "to serve the military service," "a man in service," "servant," "errand servant," etc.

甲骨文

说文『古文』

小篆

隶书

楷书

草书

行书

简化字

（同楷书）

429

# 刈 yì

〔附〕乂 yì

Its original form was written as 乂, whose form was like a mowing scissors, meaning "to mow," or "to weed." 刈 extended to express the meanings of "up-rooting," "exterminating," etc, but 乂 extended to indicate "administration," "safety and stability," "men of extraordinary talent and virtue," etc.

（同楷书）

甲骨文
金文
小篆
隶书
楷书
草书
行书
简化字

430

# 阴 (陰) yīn

Its original meaning was "on the south of the water, on the north of the mountain," hence 阳 had a radical of 阜 (left 阝). Since bronze inscriptions, there appeared many variant versions: some with 今, some with 金 as its phonetic radical, and some with 今 having 酉, 云, 虫, etc. as its lower part. The antonym of the simplified 阳 (陽) is 阴.

（缺）

陰 陰 陰 陰 陰 阴

431

# 寅 yín

〔附〕螾 yín

寅 was the original form of 螾. The original meaning was "deep." In the early oracle bone inscriptions, 矢（arrow）was used to replace 寅; only in the later oracle bone inscriptions, the form of 口 was added to the middle, indicating that the arrow had shot through the target and shot deeply. In bronze inscriptions, there appeared the form of two hands. Later, much change took place. It was often loaned to indicate the third of the Earthly Branches.

（同楷书）

432

# 引 yǐn

The grapheme in bronze inscriptions was a self-explanatory symbol being pulled outward on the bow. It meant "to pull the bow." After small seal characters, the self-explanatory symbol changed to be a vertical stroke. Later, it extended to indicate 延伸, to extend, 牵拉, to pull, 引导, to guide, etc.

| | |
|---|---|
| 甲骨文 | |
| 金文 | |
| 小篆 | |
| 隶书 | |
| 楷书 | |
| 草书 | |
| 行书 | |
| 简化字 | （同楷书） |

433

# 胤 yìn

Its initial meaning was "offspring in succession." 月 i.e. 肉, indicated the kin of one family; 幺 (meaning silk) indicated the continuous; 八 indicated branch propagation. It also referred to "offspring."

（同楷书）

434

# 应（應）yīng, yìng

〔附〕鹰（鷹）yīng

In bronze inscriptions, 鷹 was loaned to substitute for 應（应）. Its graph was like an eagle under the cliff （厂）. Later, the radical 心 was added to signify meaning; 厂 mistakenly evolved into 广 or 疒. Its initial meaning is 应当, should. When meaning 应答, respond, 顺应, conformance, 应付, cope with, it is pronounced yìng.

| 甲骨文 | 金文 | 小篆 | 隶书 | 楷书 | 草书 | 行书 | 简化字 |
|---|---|---|---|---|---|---|---|

435

# 邕 yōng

〔附〕雍 yōng 壅 yōng 饔 yōng

The original meaning was "the town surrounded by water." The character was composed of 邑 (people's living place) and 川 (rivers), an associate compound. It was interchangeable with 雝 (i.e. 雍), meaning "harmony." Later, it was loaned for use in proper terms. It was also interchangeable with 壅, 饔, etc.

| | |
|---|---|
| 甲骨文 | （缺） |
| 金文 | 〔image〕 |
| 小篆 | 〔image〕 |
| 隶书 | 〔image〕 |
| 楷书 | 邕 |
| 草书 | 〔image〕 |
| 行书 | 〔image〕 |
| 简化字 | （同楷书） |

436

# 攸 yōu

〔附〕悠 yōu

In oracle bone inscriptions, its grapheme was a hand with a tree branch hitting a person; in bronze inscriptions, the back of man in the grapheme was even blooding. 攸 was the original form of 悠, and its initial meaning was 忧愁, grief. Its significance greatly changed later on.

甲骨文

金文

小篆

隶书

楷书

草书

行书

简化字

（同楷书）

# 游（遊）yóu

It was written as 斿 originally. The original meaning was "the waving ribbons or drooping ornaments of banners in ancient times. These things were very thin and narrow, so they were expressed by 子（meaning 小, little or small）. It was also as 游. It was interchangeable with 遊 in 遨遊, roam or wonder. The simplified 游 and 遊 are both combined to 游.

（同楷书）

438

# 犹（猶）yóu

〔附〕猶 yóu

Its original significance was "a kind of monkey." It was composed of 犬 (there were no specific radicals indicating monkeys in Chinese) and 酋, indicating the pronunciation. It was the same as 猶.

# 幼 yòu

The character was made up of 力 and 幺 (the same as 糸, thin silk), signifying weak power. Its initial meaning is "young." It also refers to "children."

440

# 于 (於) yú

〔附〕迂 yū 纡(紆) yū

于 was the initial form of 迂 and 纡. Its initial meaning was 曲折, twists and turns. The earlier version was like this: by 干-shaped watercourse was a zigzag line, expressing to go round while walking. It was mostly used as a proposition and interchangeable with 於. The simplified version of 於 is replaced by 于.

| 甲骨文 | 金文 | 小篆 | 隶书 | 楷书 | 草书 | 行书 | 简化字 |
|---|---|---|---|---|---|---|---|

（同楷书）

441

# 余 yú

〔附〕馀(餘) yú

Its grapheme looks like "a dwelling place on the tree built by primitive people. Since oracle bone inscriptions, it has begun to be loaned as the first person pronoun. It was interchangeable with 馀 (餘).

（同楷书）

442

# 俞 yú

〔附〕愈 yù

The primitive meaning was "a canoe." That's to say, to make a boat by hollowing out the tree trunk. However, with the original meaning not existent, in ancient books it was often loaned as an exclamation or a family name. It was constituted of 舟 (indicating meaning) and 余 (indicating pronunciation and its form was simplified). It was also interchangeable with 愈.

甲骨文 （缺）

金文 肒

小篆 俞

隶书 俞

楷书 俞

草书 肍

行书 俞

简化字 （同楷书）

443

# 奥 yú

Its original meaning was "to tie and pull." The grapheme in bronze inscriptions was a man in the center and two hands pulling him from different side. Its initial significance is not existent, but the word 须奥 is commonly used from the ancient to the present, meaning "a very short time."

（缺）

（同楷书）

甲骨文

金文

小篆

隶书

楷书

草书

行书

简化字

444

# 予 yǔ, yú

The initial meaning was "to give," pronounced yǔ. Its grapheme was like sending something to others with the hand. It also functioned as a pronoun, the same as 我, I, pronounced yú.

（同楷书）

甲骨文

三体石经

小篆

隶书

楷书

草书

行书

简化字

# 与（與）yǔ, yù

〔附〕欤（歟）yú 举（舉）jǔ

The initial meaning was "to give." The earlier grapheme looked like a pair of hands up and a pair of hands down holding an ivory (see character 牙) and exchanging. It extended to signify 交往, contact, 参与, participate, 党与, take sides with, etc. and it was also used as a function word. It was interchangeable with 欤 and 举.

# 禹 yǔ

〔附〕龋（齲）qǔ

A hand catching a poisonous "worm," hence, that person must be a hero for having killed a vermin for the people. In ancient China, 禹, the reputed founder of the Xia Dynasty (c. 21st – 16th B.C.), was considered a hero to harness the flood. Another saying was that 禹 was "a kind of worm," so when a tooth is decayed or worm-eaten, it is called 龋（qǔ）齿.

（同楷书）

甲骨文　金文　小篆　隶书　楷书　草书　行书　简化字

# 圉 yǔ

A prisoner was cuffed and put into prison. Obviously the character meant "prison." It was also used as "a man in charge of raising horses" in ancient times.（See character 辛．）

（同楷书）

# 裕 yù

It was constituted of 衣 and 谷 ( signifying its sound ). It meant "wealthy," "abundance." The grapheme in bronze inscriptions was 衣 outside and 谷 inside; subsequently it evolved into 衣 on the left and 谷 on the right.

（缺）

（同楷书）

449

# 狱（獄）yù

The character was made up of 㹜 (yín, two dogs fighting) and 言, figuratively meaning "to dispute to suit," which was the original meaning of 狱. Its extended meanings were "criminal case," "prison," "crime," "judgement," etc.

450

# 冤 yuān

An innocent rabbit was covered (冖, meaning "to cover," pronounced mì) by something and could not move. Its original meaning is 屈缩, bend or draw back. The extended meanings are 冤枉, to wrong, 冤屈, injustice, 怨恨, hatred, 仇恨, enmity, etc.

451

# 原 yuán

〔附〕源 yuán

It was the original form of 源, meaning "the water source." Its grapheme was just like a spring（泉）under the cliff（厂）. Later, it extended to indicate "fundamental," "cause," "source," "flat land," etc.

（缺）

（同楷书）

# 龠（籥）yuè

〔附〕钥（鑰）yuè

It was an ancient musical instrument by bamboo pipes, and it seemed to be the predecessor of "line flutes," with three holes, six holes, or seven holes. It was also written as 籥. It was also a term for ancient metrology. It was interchangeable with 鑰（钥）.

（同楷书）

453

# 钺（鉞 戉）yuè

甲骨文
金文
小篆
隶书
楷书
草书
行书
简化字

It was initially written as 戉, which was just like a large axe with round blade and long handle, a pictograph. Later, the radical 金 was added and hence written as 鉞（钺）. It was also loaned for a name for a star.

454

# 勻 yún

〔附〕钧（鈞）jūn

It was the original form of 钧. It initially signified "a weight unit to measure metals." In bronze inscriptions, the exterior of the character was 旬, representing sound; in the middle was the form of two metals (see character 金), representing meaning. 勻 took on the meanings of 分出, divide and distribute, 均勻, equality.

（同楷书）

455

# 允 yǔn

Its graphemes in oracle bone inscriptions and bronze inscriptions were both like a person nodding his head to express his belief. The original meaning was "to believe." It was mostly used to check the result of divination, i.e. 果然, as expected. Its extended meanings were 允许, permission, 公平, fair.

（同楷书）

456

# 孕 yùn

The grapheme of 孕 in oracle bone inscriptions certainly took the shape of a woman being pregnant. However, since the Warring States Period its grapheme has become dissimilar to its origin. It extended to signify 孕育, gestate.

（同楷书）

457

# 晕（暈）yùn, yūn

The original meaning is "the light circles around the sun or the moon," which is formed by the reflection of icy crystals in the clouds when the sunlight or the moonlight goes through. In oracle bone inscriptions, it was like the sun halo. Since small seal characters, there appeared a phonogram 暈. Later, it was loaned for describing the symptom of being dizzy or unconscious.

（缺）

458

# 载（載）zài, zǎi

The primitive meaning was "to load." It was composed of 车 (indicating its meaning) and 𢦏 (zāi, indicating its sound). It extended to signify 承受, stand, 担负, shoulder, 放置, put or place, etc. (pronounced zài). It also signified 记录, note, 年岁, ages or years, such as 载入史册, go down in history, 三年五载, three years or five years, (pronounced zǎi).

甲骨文

金文

小篆

隶书

楷书

草书

行书

简化字

459

# 赞 (贊讚) zàn

Its upper part was 兟（shēn）, meaning "to enter"（two 先 side by side meaning "striving to be first"）；贝 was considered ancient currency in ancient times. When joined together it means to see an important person with a present of 贝. It originally meant "to see." It extends to signify 辅佐, assist，帮助, help. Its variant version 讚 now has been combined to 赞.

460

# 葬 zàng

Its original meaning was "to bury the dead body." Its grapheme in oracle bone inscriptions was a dead body in the coffin buried under the earth and grass already grew up. The graph in small seal characters was a character of 死 in the center and the grass up and down.

（同楷书）

461

# 枣（棗）zǎo

枣树, jujube, is a kind of defoliating arbor, which is characteristic of upright branches and curve thorns. Hence, the grapheme in bronze inscriptions took the shape of many thorns; in small seal characters it evolved into two 朿（cì, i.e. 刺 in ancient times）, which was much pictographic. The lower 朿 of the simplified version has been replaced by ㇇ (repetition symbol).

（缺）

甲骨文

金文

小篆

隶书

楷书

草书

行书

简化字

462

# 蚤 zǎo

〔附〕早 zǎo

In ancient times, the pest that people met mostly was flea, hence, a hand and an "amplified" pest were loaned to signify the character of 蚤. In addition, it was also loaned to substitute for 早 in ancient books.

（缺）

（同楷书）

# 早 zǎo

〔附〕蚤 zǎo

（缺）

（同楷书）

The sun（日）was shinning on the helmets（甲）and it was time for soldiers to get up in the morning. 早 means morning, composed of 日 above 甲. 蚤 was loaned for use as 早 in ancient writings（see character 蚤）.

# 噪 zào

On the tree were three (signifying many) mouths shouting (should be bird beaks rather than man's mouths). 喿 was the original form of 噪. The original meaning is "the birds' noisy calling."

465

# 灶 (竈) zào

〔附〕造 zào

The original meaning is the device for burning or cooking food, built by laying earth and bricks or other things. It was made up of 穴 (for the stove with a burning opening) and 黽 (today pronounced cù, i.e. toad, indicating sound but its form simplified). Again, it was loaned for use as 厨房, kitchen. In bronze inscriptions and ancient books, it was sometimes interchangeable with 造. The simplified version is written as 灶.

466

# 则 （則） zé

The character was originally composed of 刀, knife, and 鼎, tripod, meaning to scribe characters of rules or codes on a tripod for later generations to obey. Its original meanings were 准则, rules, and 法典, codes. It extended to mean 效仿, to follow the fashion of, and as a function word.

甲骨文

金文

小篆

隶书

楷书

草书

行书

简化字

# 贼（賊）zéi

It was not a phonogram but an associate compound. It was composed of 人,
戈 and 贝, signifying that a hand with
weapons destroyed a precious cowrie（as
currency by ancient people）. Its original
meaning was "to destroy." It extended to
indicate 伤害, damage or hurt, 杀害,
kill or murder, 逆乱者, traitors, 盗贼,
robbers, etc.

（缺）

468

# 曾 zēng，céng

〔附〕甑 zèng 增 zēng 层（層）céng

曾 was the original form of 甑 (zèng). This was a kitchen utensil for cooking food, which had some small ventilating holes in the middle layer, just like today's steam box. It was mostly loaned for use as a function word, therefore, another character 甑 was coined to convey the original meaning. 曾 was sometimes interchangeable with 增 and 层（層）.

| 甲骨文 |
| 金文 |
| 小篆 |
| 隶书 |
| 楷书 |
| 草书 |
| 行书 |
| 简化字 |

（同楷书）

# 宅 zhái

宅 is the dwelling place where people live, i.e. a dwelling house. It was initially made up of 宀 (the form of house) and 乇 (indicating sound). 乇, pronounced zhé today, was a grass. It extended to indicate 居住, dwell, 居于, inhabit, or be (in a certain position or place), 处于, be in a certain condition (or state), etc.

（同楷书）

470

# 章 zhāng

The original meaning is 标记, marker. In bronze inscriptions, the character of 章 was just like a punishment knife（辛）scribing circular marks on slave soldiers. Since small seal characters, it mistakenly changed to be 音 and 十, which is not understandable.

（缺）

（同楷书）

# 丈 zhàng

〔附〕杖 zhàng

丈 was the original form of 杖, which looked like a hand taking a stick or something. But why there used to a change in official script, see character 支 for reference: since 𰻝 (支) in small seal characters could be written as 支, then 𰻝 (丈) wouldn't be identical in small seal characters. One 丈 equals to 十尺 (about 3.3 meters); it also means 丈夫, husband, and others.

| | |
|---|---|
| 甲骨文 | （缺） |
| 金文 | （缺） |
| 小篆 | |
| 隶书 | |
| 楷书 | |
| 草书 | |
| 行书 | |
| 简化字 | （同楷书） |

472

# 朝 zhāo, cháo

Its original meaning is 早晨, morning. The grapheme in oracle bone inscriptions looked like the sun just rising over the grass and the moon not disappearing yet completely. The right radical of the character changed a great deal: it was the water-shape in bronze inscriptions; the form of 舟 in small seal characters; the form of 月 after official script. Later, it extended to mean 朝见, meet with a king or emperor, 朝廷, the court, 朝代, dynasty, in which 朝 is pronounced cháo.

| | |
|---|---|
| 甲骨文 | |
| 金文 | |
| 小篆 | |
| 隶书 | |
| 楷书 | |
| 草书 | |
| 行书 | （同楷书） |
| 简化字 | |

473

# 兆 zhào

The ancient people burned the shell of a tortoise to see the crack shapes for predicting good or bad fortune, and these cracks were called 兆. In bronze inscriptions, it was constituted of a few of arc lines, signifying the way of divination. It extended to mean 预兆, omen, etc.

（同楷书）

474

# 照 zhào

The original meaning is "to shine." Graphically in bronze inscriptions, it was a hand（又）raising a tree branch with 火, fire, on it; 召 indicates sound（see character 召）. Since small seal characters, it had 日 and 火 as graphic radicals. After official script, 火 changed to be 灬.

475

肇 zhào

The original meaning was "to start." Historically, it had many written forms. In oracle bone inscriptions, it was like an ancient dagger thrusting a window, i.e. starting to attack the castle or town. In bronze inscriptions, some version was like a hand pulling out the latch, signifying the door just being opened. In official script and regular script, there appeared a couple of versions such as 肁, 肇, 肇. Today, 肇 is regarded as the standard character.

| 甲骨文 |
| 金文 |
| 小篆 |
| 隶书 |
| 楷书 |
| 草书 |
| 行书 |
| 简化字 |

（同楷书）

476

# 哲（喆）zhé

（缺）

（同楷书）

The original meaning was 明智, in reason, extensively referring to wise people. In bronze inscriptions, it was mostly made up of 心, 斤 (the variant form of 折); 折 indicates being able to convince people and also indicates sound. Since small seal characters, it has been written as 哲. However, in official script and regular script, it had a variant version of 喆. Today's standard version is 哲.

# 者 zhě

〔附〕蔗 zhè 诸（諸）zhū

者 was the original form of 藷 or 蔗. The upper part of the character in bronze inscriptions was a sugarcane with both stalk and leaves, and a couple of dots signified the cane juice; the lower was 口 or 甘（甜, sweet）. Later, it was mostly loaned for use as a function word. It was interchangeable with 诸, such as 者侯.

甲骨文

金文

小篆

隶书

楷书

草书

行书

简化字

（同楷书）

478

# 争 zhēng

〔附〕诤（諍）zhèng

Two hands up and down were struggling for something like an ox horn. The original meaning was 争夺, contend for, 夺取, capture. It extended to mean 辩论, debate, 竞争, compete, etc. It was interchangeable with 诤, meaning "to expostulate with," such as 争（诤）友.

甲骨文

（缺）

金文

小篆

隶书

楷书

草书

行书

简化字

（同楷书）

479

# 支 zhī

〔附〕枝 zhī 肢 zhī

It is the original form of 枝. Its primitive grapheme was a hand grasping a bamboo branch. It extended to indicate 分支，branch，支出，disburse，支持，support，干支 and 四支（later as 肢），four limbs，etc.

（同楷书）

480

# 制（製）zhì

The original meaning was "cut off." The character was made up of 刀 and 未. 未 meant flourishing, and the trees can only be felled only after they grew up so as to be processed for wooden products. It still contained the significance of 制作, make, 制造, manufacture, and was later written 製. Today, 制 has replaced as 製 in simplified versions.

（缺）

（同楷书）

甲骨文

金文

小篆

隶书

楷书

草书

行书

简化字

481

豸 zhì

（缺）

（同楷书）

The original meaning was "beasts of long backbones," e.g. cats, tigers, etc. 豺, jackal, 貂, ermine, 豹, leopard, 貉, racoon dog, etc. all have the same radical of 豸. Later, it also referred to footless worms, such as earthworms and others.

# 志（誌）zhì

〔附〕识（識）zhì, shí

It was originally composed of 心 and 之 indicating its pronunciation. Its phonetic radical was written as 之（i.e. 止）before, and after official script it mistakenly turned out to be 士 or 土. It mostly indicated the meanings of 志愿, will, and 志向, ideal. It also had the meanings of 意会, sense, 心情, feeling, 神志, consciousness, etc. It was interchangeable with 识（識）and 誌.

甲骨文（缺）

金文

小篆

隶书

楷书

草书

行书

简化字（同楷书）

483

炙 zhì

It originally meant "to roast meats." Its constitution was 肉, meat, above 火, fire. It also referred to "meat which was already well burned or roasted." It was still a method of Chinese medicine making, i.e. to fry together medical materials with supplement juicy materials, such as 蜜炙.

（缺）

（同楷書）

# 彘 zhì

Its original meaning was "a wild boar." The earlier grapheme was a boar shot by an arrow, signifying that it was apparently not a domestic animal. Later, it also referred to a pig.

甲骨文

金文

小篆

隶书

楷书

草书

行书

简化字

（同楷书）

485

# 重 zhòng, chóng

The character was originally made up of 人 and 东, among which man's weight was loaned to indicate meaning, i.e. to indicate 重 in 轻重, indicating how heavy something is, and 东 was only referring to its sound. It extended to indicate "tight," "thick," "respect," "increase," etc. In addition, it is pronounced chóng when meaning 重复, repetition, 重叠, overlap, 再, again, and so on.

東 鼉 重 重 全 全

（同楷书）

# 冑 zhòu

It was a headgear for soldiers to protect their heads in ancient times and called 盔, helmet, later on. Its upper part in bronze inscriptions was quite like the shape of a helmet; its lower was 目, signifying the head. Later, the upper became 由 and the lower 月 mistakenly, hence it confused itself with 胄, which had been composed of 肉 and 月 (indicating sound), originally meaning "the offspring of emperors, kings, or peerage."

| | |
|---|---|
| 甲骨文 | （缺） |
| 金文 | |
| 小篆 | |
| 隶书 | |
| 楷书 | |
| 草书 | |
| 行书 | |
| 简化字 | （同楷书） |

487

# 昼（晝）zhòu

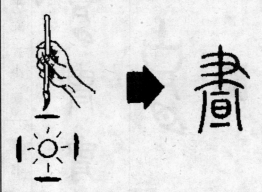

It means "daytime." Its upper part was 聿, i.e. 笔; the lower were 日 and a few lines, signifying the division of the period between the sunrise and the sunset, i.e. between day and night.

# 蛛 zhū

In bronze inscriptions, it was written as 鼄, composing of 黽 and 朱 (indicating sound). But in small seal characters, 鼄 was thought of an official version and 蛛 a variant. (蜘 in small seal characters was written as 蠤, not found in bronze inscriptions). 蛛 means 蜘蛛, spider.

（缺）

（同楷书）

甲骨文

金文

小篆

隶书

楷书

草书

行书

简化字

# 竹 zhú

As a pictograph, it looked like two plants of bamboo side by side with their leaves drooped. It also referred to 竹简, bamboo slips for writing on. In ancient times, it also indicated bamboo musical instruments like 箫, a vertical bamboo flute, 笛, a bamboo flute, i.e. one of 八音, eight kinds of musical instruments.

（缺）

（同楷书）

# 主 zhǔ

〔附〕炷 zhù

主 was the original form of 炷, meaning 灯心, lampwick. In ancient times kindling was very precious and it was in custody of the chief of a tribe, hence, it was loaned to indicate a leader. Later, it extended to mean 君主, king or emperor, 主人, host, 主持, preside, etc.

甲骨文

（缺）

三体石经

小篆

隶书

楷书

草书

行书

简化字

（同楷书）

491

# 箸 zhù

〔附〕著 zhù 着 zhuó

箸，著，着，these three charac-
ters, came from the same origin. It could
be interchangeable with one another in
ancient writings, but today they are quite
different. Of 箸，竹 indicates the significance, 者（sounding familiar with that
of 诸 in ancient times）indicates sound,
and its original meaning was "chop-
sticks." Some of the significance items of
箸 were subsequently written as 著，and
著 to 着 in the same way.

492

# 专（專）zhuān

〔附〕转（轉）zhuǎn, zhuàn

专 was the original form of 转. Graphically in oracle bone inscriptions, it was like a hand spinning 叀（纺专, i.e. spindles）. While spinning the spindles the cotton wool would spin into yarn, or yarn into thread.

甲骨文

金文

小篆

隶书

楷书

草书

行书

简化字

# 缀（綴）zhuì

As a pictograph, it was written as 叕, meaning "to join," or it had 糸 as a radical. The original meaning is 缝补, sew and mend, 缝合, stitch. It extends to mean 连结, coupling, 装饰, decorating, etc.

# 卓 zhuó

〔附〕罩 zhào 桌 zhuó

卓 was the original form of 罩. Graphically in oracle bone inscriptions, its lower part was a net with a long handle (see character 毕); the upper part a simplified version of 鸟, bird. The initial meaning was "to net a bird." Because the bird is flying high in the sky, it has a meaning of 高, high. It was interchangeable with 桌 (which is a later developed character).

（同楷书）

# 字 zì

The original meaning was "to give birth to." It extended to indicate 出嫁, get married, 怀孕, be pregnant, 养育, bring up, etc. It is still loaned to mean 文字, written language, 名字, name, etc.

（缺）

（同楷书）

甲骨文
金文
小篆
隶书
楷书
草书
行书
简化字

# 走 zǒu

（缺）

In bronze inscriptions, graphically 走 and 奔 (see character 奔) were both the same form as a man running in their upper parts; the difference was that under the character of 走 was only one foot (止，i.e. 趾) and under 奔 three feet. Hence, 走 signified "running," and 奔 signified "rapidly running."

甲骨文

金文

小篆

隶书

楷书

草书

行书

简化字

（同楷书）

497

# 最 zuì

The original meaning was "to offend and take away." It was originally made up of 冃 (帽子, hat, see character 帽) and 取, meaning to offend another and take his hat away. With its original meaning not existent any longer, it often refers to people with high positions, superior military or political achievements. It is mostly used as an adverb.

甲骨文 （缺）

秦简文 寂

小篆 扇

隶书 宴

楷书 最

草书 㝡

行书 最

简化字 （同楷书）

498

# 罪（辠）zuì

辠 was the original form of 罪. 自 meant a nose, and 辛 meant a punishment knife, which together meant "to cut off a nose with a knife and punish the guilty people." 罪 is composed of 罒 (i.e. 网, the arm of the law) and 非 (unlawful persons).

甲骨文

（缺）

金文

辠

小篆

罪

隶书

罪

楷书

辠

草书

罪

行书

（同楷书）

简化字

499

# 坐 zuò

〔附〕座 zuò

坐 takes the form of two persons face to face sitting on the ground. The ancient people at first sat on the ground and later changed to sit in chairs or on benches. It extends to indicate 留守, stay to take care of, 获罪, be guilty, 居住, reside in, 坐位（also as 座位）, seat.

（缺）

甲骨文

说文『古文』

坐

小篆

坐

隶书

坐

楷书

坐

草书

坐

行书

（同楷书）

简化字